COSMIC!

BERKSHIRE

Edited by Simon Harwin

First published in Great Britain in 1999 by
POETRY NOW YOUNG WRITERS
1-2 Wainman Road, Woodston,
Peterborough, PE2 7BU
Telephone (01733) 230748

HB ISBN 0 754301 672
SB ISBN 0 754301 680

FOREWORD

With over 63,000 entries for this year's Cosmic competition, it has proved to be our most demanding editing year to date.

We were, however, helped immensely by the fantastic standard of entries we received, and, on behalf of the Young Writers team, thank you.

The Cosmic series is a tremendous reflection on the writing abilities of 8-11 year old children, and the teachers who have encouraged them must take a great deal of credit.

We hope that you enjoy reading *Cosmic Berkshire* and that you are impressed with the variety of poems and style with which they are written, giving an insight into the minds of young children and what they think about the world today.

Contents

Sandy Lane Junior School

The Hawthorns Primary School		
	Michael Logan	150
	Nadia Leathes	150
	Nathan Elcox	151
	Gregg Allison	151
	Celeste Griffiths	151
	Jessica Crandon	152
Uplands Primary School		
	Laura Miller	152
	Holly Yapp	153
	Christopher Hammersley	153
	Alex Todd	154
	Lee Burnett	154
	Jade Iehec Watson	155
	Kelly Head	155
	Aaron Morgan	156
	Charlotte Rough	156
	Amiirah Joommun	157
	Mikayla Field	158
	Lucy Fuller	158
	Daniel Smith	159
	Thomas Evans	159
	Natalie Cobbett	160
	Ashley Jones	160
	Daniel Deller-Twinney	161
	Georgina Brown	162
	Luke Groves	162
	Laura Cobbett	163
Waverley School		
	Amy Lack	164
	Andrew Sinclair	164
	Matthew Edwards	165
	Paul Stephenson	165
	Faye Hetherington	166
	Jay McCafferty	167
	Caroline Hoad	167

THE POEMS

OPPOSITE SEX

Opposites, different, we're never the same
We will always be different
Nothing you can say
Nothing you can do
Will ever change them
Everywhere we go all that you see
All that you hear are them.
The opposite sex all around us getting closer
Every minute every second of the day
They're watching, looking, never touching
Just always there, never going, never fading.
They will always be there, the opposite sex.
Opposite different we're never the same
We will always be different.

Kirsty Brown

THE CLEAR WORLD!

Last night I had a dream,
I dreamt the world,
Was as clear as cream,
Not on the street were there any bombs,
Not on the street were there any peeping Toms,
Not on the street were there any people sleeping,
Not on the street were there any people weeping,
The world was full of wonderful peace,
As so the world had no thieves,
I woke up and saw the light,
The world was the same,
It was just a fright.

Bina Thakrar (10)

SURROUNDING WORLD

When the world that surrounds you starts crumbling apart,
When all there is, is a finish when there should've been a start,
When misty gloomy weather troubled days fall on your head,
When the new day comes around again but you don't make it out of bed.

When the scenes you see around you of misery, sadness and pain,
You really start to wonder if there's a point to try again.
You think of all the good then of all the bad,
Suddenly all the good seems lost and you feel oh so sad.

The world is really losing perhaps already lost,
But we've got to keep on fighting we have at any cost.
The windows in our life are shattering in front of you,
But we seem to be just sitting with nothing left to do.

I just don't understand why we're all still suffering this life,
We seem to be sitting putting up with loneliness and strife.

Erica Holloway

SPRING

Now that it is warm and sunny spring,
I can go out and play on the swing,
Spring is when the flowers start to grow,
And summer will come before we know.

Animals wake from their winter sleep,
All winter they did not give a peep.
The winter days are no longer grey,
New born lambs and bunnies play all day.

Sandeep Kaur Gill (10)
All Saints CE Primary School

MOTHER'S DAY

On Mother's Day you should get whatever you want,
Never be horrible because your mum might get upset.
You should treat your mother with respect,
Mother's Day is important because it's a day
That is special to your mum.

Nikita Dulai (7)
All Saints CE Primary School

CHIPS

Chips are
   crinkly
      wrinkly
         with
      ketchup and mustard
   salt
and
   vinegar
      on
         the
            top!
They're crispy
   on the
      outside
         and
      yummy
   on the
in!

David Sewell (9)
All Saints CE Primary School

CHILDREN AND PARENTS

Parents always nag,
Children always make a mess,
And when their parents find out,
The children always hide.
But when their parents find them,
The children are sent to bed without their supper.

Parents take you on a treat,
Because they are feeling generous,
But there is one problem,
The children of course,
The children ask for this and that,
When parents don't have any cash.

The children can be horrible,
So can parents,
The children can be helpful,
But I am not sure about parents.
Children and parents don't go together,
And sometimes they do.

Some children think their parents don't love them.
But they do
Parents can't live without their children,
Children can't live without their parents.

Hasnaat Iftekhar (10)
All Saints CE Primary School

THE WASHING MACHINE

Once you
put your clothes in
turn on to

Load

round and round
chewing,
gurgling,
churning,
up and down.
An opening porthole
in a
square based body.
Crunching,
munching,
moaning,
groaning,
until the munching monster falls asleep,
dead and motionless.

Ping

Then comes a shout,
Mum says,
'Get that washing out.'

Samuel Headlong-Moore (9)
All Saints CE Primary School

The Scary Aeroplane

A huge smooth oval shape
Two humungous clear shiny eyes
A pair of the longest arms in the world
And a tail with incy wincy legs just below.
But
At night it turns into a fierce dragon.
The tail grows and has a point.
Its mouth wide open,
Teeth glittering in the moonlight,
Eyes as fierce as can be.
Its legs disappear and then away it flies.

Mathew Herbert (9)
All Saints CE Primary School

Mother's Day

When it was Mother's Day I gave my mummy a present.
All the time I loved her I never said I didn't.
Mother's Day is special because it's a time for you
to be happy that you have a mother.
A mother always cares about you so you should
treat her with respect.
The colour red is the colour of love
because you love them with your heart.
So if you're doing something with love
it's loving if you use the colour red.

Anisha Seth (8)
All Saints CE Primary School

The Reason Why Elephants . . .

The reason why elephants fly,
Is because they have ease,
On the flying trapeze.
They soar through the air,
Without a single care,
And that is why
Elephants fly!

The reason why elephants cry,
Is because they take too much
space,
In the wonderful animal race.
They try to fit in,
But they're not really thin,
And that is why
Elephants cry!

The reason why
Most elephants lie,
Is because they don't want
to be like Ruth
(A goody-goody elephant)
Who always, always tells the
truth.
They lie and talk,
While taking a walk.
And that is why
Elephants lie!

Jenny Boyd (11)
All Saints CE Primary School

The Cat I Had

I had this cat
for years, years and years.

I has this cat when it was born
for years, years and years.

I had this cat when I was born
for years, years and years.

I had this cat when I was six months
for years, years and years.

I washed this cat
for years, years and years.

I kept this cat
for years, years and years.

I kept this cat for twelve years
for years, years and years.

And now my cat is dead!

Sarah Logie (9)
All Saints CE Primary School

Star Flight

The spaceship is zooming through the stars
Faster than lightning!
Planets are floating in space.

It is amazing up here
You have to eat weird food
We've hit a few rocks on the journey.

We are about 100 kilometres from the moon
The trip is very rough
You can get rather sick
I've seen about 10 shooting stars
Here comes the captain
We are just about to land on the moon.

It was a rough landing
But we're fine
Now we're going to do our experiments.

Peter Deal (10)
All Saints CE Primary School

SPACE

Diving deep, jumping high
To the moon across the sky.

Diving, driving high and low,
Jump into the rocket and off we go.

Asteroids, aliens way up high
In the pitch black sky,
Nothing else gets that high.

Bits and bobs floating up,
From the world down below us.

We travel past planets - Zog and Mars,
Didn't see much, we were going too fast.

We stopped to talk to Zig and Zag,
They gave us a dirty piece of bag.

Time to go back to Earth,
See you next time, I fly.

Justine Ray (10)
All Saints CE Primary School

Christmas Time

Santa, O Santa do not forget me, I've left you mince pies under the tree.
Fill my stocking right to the brim and please bring me a money tin.
O Santa, O Santa have a safe flight
I know you will be travelling all through the night.
Without Rudolph guiding the sleigh
Santa you will never find your way.
I hear the bells of the reindeer jingling as you go over people's houses,
As you come down the chimney I can hear the bag of toys
rumbling together.
Early in the morning the children come down to open their presents.
Thank you o thank you for all the presents you give.
I shall see you next year, I hope!

Sureeta Lota (10)
All Saints CE Primary School

Hedgehogs

Hedgehogs are prickly,
They eat worms and slugs,
They curl up when danger comes,
But they can never save themselves when cars come,
They hibernate over winter,
They have smooth faces, hairy tummies and they are quite rough,
They move very slowly,
They are very small, but sometimes they're big.

Hannah Burgess (8)
All Saints CE Primary School

The Octopus

Deep down under the sea,
The octopus looked at me,
With his eight long legs
And his big oval eyes
Gosh he is a big size.

Hunting for his prey,
Searching all day,
Then a bit of luck,
Caught a baby squid for his tuck.

His soft slimy skin squirming all around,
The tentacles nearly touching the ground,
Sliming all over the rocks,
Banging his round head on the dock,

Killing himself on an anchor
Before he tried to thank her,
Sinking down down down far away,
Maybe we can watch his ghost another day.

Melanie Joel (9)
All Saints CE Primary School

Summer

In summer I like playing in the hot sun.
I like playing in the garden when the sun is shining bright.
I like feeling the cool breeze run through my hair.
I like to lie down and sunbathe in the heat of the sun.
I like sucking a cool ice-lolly,
I can feel it dripping down my chest.
When the sun slowly sets the day peacefully ends.

Gulzaar Barn (7)
All Saints CE Primary School

Seasons

Spring has sprung,
The sheep have begun,
To give birth to young lambs,
While we play in the park.

Spring is done,
Summer has begun,
Leaves fall off the trees,
Kids play conker matches.

While autumn runs away,
Winter gets colder every day,
Snow starts to fall,
People build snowmen.

Spring, summer, autumn, winter,
Every season in the year,
Don't sit down and have a beer,
Play outside all day.

Kiran Arora (10)
All Saints CE Primary School

Dolphin Deep

Across the floor of the bright sea bed,
Over seaweed, shells thousands of miles deep,
Rocks with spots of mildew and sand,
Dolphin deep swimming round and round.

The fish with their shiny fins,
Looking for something good to eat,
Boats and rubber rings floating and,
Zooming across the surface.
Forward backwards round and round,
Dolphin deep, swimming round and round,

Down we go in a submarine,
Faster than rockets taking off in the wind,
'Whoosh' goes the water 'Roar' go the waves,
Going over rocks like wheels on a train,
All kinds of fish, orange, purple and green,
Still the dolphin deep swimming round and round.

The moon is up, the sun goes down,
Relaxing on the beach all day long,
Down under the sea shadows of . . .
Dolphin deep going round and round.

Phillipa Hodgson (9)
All Saints CE Primary School

THE SNAKE

Snakes are scary, snakes are smooth
Not slimy, slippery, rough or rude.
Tree snakes tangled up in twigs.
Those silly things like long thin pigs.

Puff adders slither along the sand,
Never slipping, sliding, spinning or squirming.
Cobras spit a deadly poison,
Killing rabbits, birds and prey.

Rattlesnakes sidewind across the sand,
Scaring off predators trying to pounce.
Panthers hiding in the shadows.
Viper ready to kill its prey
And sink its jaws into flesh.

Andrew Boyd (10)
All Saints CE Primary School

STAR TREK

The starship Enterprise zooming through space!
Firing their phasers around space,
Around the galaxy!

Captain Kirk is in command
Going faster than the speed of light!
Around the galaxy!

The Klingons are coming
Fire the torpedoes
Bang bang bang
Around the galaxy!

Starfleet signal the Enterprise back
But Captain Kirk refuses to come back,
Around the galaxy!

Probes are firing to somewhere no one knows?
Looking for data about space,
Around the galaxy!

Daniel Klinker (10)
All Saints CE Primary School

THE FAIR

The grass is bare,
Now the brass fair has gone.

Gone, gone far away
It won't come back till another day.
There're sweet wrappers everywhere,
It'll take more than today to clear away.

Gone gone far away
When it's wet everywhere,
You'd better beware
'Cause there are wrappers everywhere
Of the winners.
In the candyfloss fair,
Gone gone far away.

Georgina Palmer (10)
All Saints CE Primary School

The Tunnel Of Love!

The tunnel of love
Is for me and you
It's flowing with hearts red and blue

It can be red it can be blue
As long as we can make it through

So come with me
I'll make it worth it
But only if you come with me
In the tunnel of love.

Let's go and have some fun
In the tunnel of love
And see the parts of our broken hearts

So now we've been in the
Tunnel of love
Let's start something new
Like making a tunnel of love
On our own!

Melissa May (9)
All Saints CE Primary School

My Bunk Bed

My bunk bed is huge.
I sleep on the top
And my brother sleeps on the bottom.
It stands in the corner of my room.
In the night,
When it's quiet and dark
My bunk bed turns into a double decker bus!
The engine starts up,
It drives out of my bedroom,
Across the landing,
Down the stairs
And out of the door . . .
But
When the clock strikes twelve
It returns home.
It is my bunk bed once again.

Harpreet Sarah (9)
All Saints CE Primary School

The Morning Light

I open the curtains,
And feel the heat,
Of the golden morning light.

Its wonderful grace,
As it shows its face,
Rising up into the sky.

But the clouds in the sky,
Come creeping by,
Trying to hide the beautiful light.

So at night we say goodbye,
To the golden morning light,
But we're not sad we're really glad,
That it'll come again tomorrow!

Catriona Sutter (9)
All Saints CE Primary School

MY RECORDER

My recorder is brown and smooth.
It has nine small round black holes
along its body.
The small round holes are black beady eyes
staring back at me.
It just lies there lifeless
until air is breathed into the small slit
in its end.
Suddenly it comes to life
and sings its own shrill whistling tune.
First it goes from high to low
then low to high.
Its thin brown body bringing life to the room.
At last its shrill whistly tune dies down
and it goes back into its slim leather case,
lifeless once more.

Nicola Hine (9)
All Saints CE Primary School

THE FAIRIES

Fairies fly with wings like glass,
Their curly hair looks just like brass,
They swoop and glide with all their grace
Bringing joy to many a place.

They may be fast, they may be slow,
They'll follow you wherever you go.
Not everyone can see them though
You have to believe to see that glow.

The glow appears when they're around,
Fairy dust sprinkles to the ground.
So keep on looking, and you might see
The magic fairies that visit me.

Stephanie Davis (10)
All Saints CE Primary School

THE LOVELY DAY

It was a lovely day in May
Today was hot I needed a pot of water
Today is a lovely day for me
I wish it was winter because it snows in winter
Tomorrow is a very good day for me
Because it's nearly time to go to Spain
Today is a lovely day for me.

Martin Perkins (7)
All Saints CE Primary School

THE MONSTER IN THE GARAGE

The bonnet's open and lights are flashing
It looks like a monster hiding in the night
Its huge black round feet
And its shiny shoes seem quite neat
But worst of all
Is its bright navy skin
Covering its stretched body.
Its just standing there waiting . . .
To be unlocked with a click.

Roger Towersey (9)
All Saints CE Primary School

THE STICK TREE

It's tall and brown.
It's got spikes coming out like rough sharp
Pointed fingers.
This brown monster sleeps outside
my window ledge.
Its huge body staring in at me!
Its sharp black teeth, big bulgy eyes
and scary nose peep through my window.
It's spooky when I look at it.
It moves slightly in the night air.
It seems to grow and grow every day.
Will it ever stop?

Claire Darby (8)
All Saints CE Primary School

A Fighter Jet

The green and brown painted plane
With its British air force signs
has two big bulging engines.
The magnificent white writing says
'Harriet jet number 34896'
Under the wings are twelve bombs
ready to drop!
The complicated cockpit
has millions of buttons and gadgets.
It lies on the HMS Invincible,
as if it could never do anything.
In raging battle, firing missiles
and swerving
it looks like a fiercesome dragon
flashing through the night.

Stuart Ratcliffe (8)
All Saints CE Primary School

Lions And Tigers

Tigers are fierce, powerful and strong,
They have teeth that are very very long,
Lions are lazy they sleep all day,
They are really quite clever did you know that by the way?
When they're catching animals they are sometimes wrong,
And when they're sleeping they can smell like a pong.

Caspar Algar (9)
Cheapside CE Primary School

Monkey Business

Give me back my sandwich,
Hey you come back here now.
I'll have to eat a banana then,
Oh no not you again now.
I hate those silly monkeys,
They play and play all day.
Can I have my lunch back now,
Or will I have to pay?

Charlotte Ellis (9)
Cheapside CE Primary School

Dancing Dragons

Dancing dragons are so funny,
they don't even know that bears eat honey.
They dance and dance to entertain
the rabbits
but for all the dancing dragons,
to entertain is such a pain,
and you would have thought
that dancing dragons are so silly,
well you would have been right
because one of the dancing dragons
called Billy
went down the road on a cheetah
to see his sister Milly.

Emily Nokes (9)
Cheapside CE Primary School

OWLS

An owl was swooping through the night,
It wanted something that it could bite.
Dark shadows glided through the trees,
Flying past a swarm of bees.
Suddenly something caught his eye,
When he was flying very high.
He caught a small mouse,
And flew back to his house.
The owl sat ready to eat,
With the small mouse asleep on his feet.

Laura Brennand-Carter (9)
Cheapside CE Primary School

DANCING PIGS

Dancing pigs are so silly,
They dance and dance and make themselves dizzy.
My pig is called Busy because
He spends all his time being silly,
His friend Billy always dances and gets
Dizzy
Dizzy
Dizzy
Dizzy
Dizzy!

Rochelle Rekowski (8)
Cheapside CE Primary School

The Robin

When I was walking on my way
I saw a robin in some hay
I said to him 'How do you do?'
He said back 'I've got the flu.'
I said to him 'If you don't
Feel at your best
You'd better rest.'
'Oh you are so kind
You must think of me in your mind.'

Amy Spencer (8)
Cheapside CE Primary School

My Goldfish

The shimmering shadow of my goldfish,
Is something you would like to see,
He slides and slides and smoothly swims,
In the pond so clear.
My glistening goldfish,
Is so nice to see,
I like him and so I see he likes me.

Charlotte Humphreys (9)
Cheapside CE Primary School

Leopard

Fast running
Lies down
Never goes in water or it will drown.
Up and down again.
Ready to catch
But dinner runs past again
Hungry leopard goes for his grassy patch.

Jessica Allan (8)
Cheapside CE Primary School

Giraffes

Giraffes eat the juicy leaves off the trees,
They have long necks that help them see,
They run a mile across the grass,
They stop to eat a bunch of leaves.

Sarah Holmes (8)
Cheapside CE Primary School

Koala

Koala climbing bravely holding onto the branches.
Koala roughly clinging on branches a very long way down.
Higher and higher, up and up stopping resting and eating.
Then down and down, lower and lower it goes
Back down the tree.

Alice Allan (8)
Cheapside CE Primary School

Elephants And Tigers

Elephants are big, fat and strong,
They have tusks big and long.

Tigers are powerful and strong,
But they are not long.
Their teeth are very sharp and they are dark.

Jonathan Gurr (9)
Cheapside CE Primary School

What Am I?

I'm that something in the water,
I make you shout and scream,
No one is like me,
No one likes me,
You never get the message,
Stay away from lakes!
I'll eat anyone's flesh and bone,
You can't stop me doing that,
Ducks and chimps I sometimes get,
Stay away or I'll eat you up,
Anyway my name rhymes with iguana.

Pavan Dhillon (8)
Cippenham Middle School

Friends

F riends make you comfortable
R unning around in a game
I have friends all around me
E very morning waiting for me
N ew friends have been made
D angerous times they are with you
S o many I cannot count.

Sangeetha Rajan (7)
Cippenham Middle School

Summertime

S ummer is beautiful and wonderful things happen
U nicorns run wild across the poppy field
M e, yes I am having a wonderful time
M y cat is getting lost in the daffodil garden next door
E gg sandwiches are being made for picnics
R abbits love it and so do I.

Melanie Diggle (8)
Cippenham Middle School

I Am A Tiger

I am a tiger all furry and tall
I have sharp teeth and long claws
I live in the jungles of Asia and India
My teeth are made for ripping my food
My claws are for holding my food
And for climbing trees to hunt for my prey
You must not pet me
I will bite you and scratch you
Tiger tiger in the night with my eyes burning bright.

Tristan Ross-Barnard (8)
Cippenham Middle School

How To Paint A Picture Of Spring

Take the canvas of life and the brush of creation,
The paints of hope and water of damnation;
Now you have the set of tools worthy of a king,
It's time to paint your picture of spring.

Dab flowers to the left and joy to the right,
Add a child at play and a shaft of sunlight;
Open all the bright yellows and gold,
And hide all the colours of sadness and cold.

With a brush stroke that's lighter than air,
You create a masterpiece worthy of care;
A picture of happiness and life new born,
Of spring; each new year's dawn.

Tom Godfrey (11)
Courthouse Junior School

WINTER DAYS

Winter days so crisp and cold,
Glassy, icy, shimmering ponds,
Frozen leaves stuck to the path,
Snow covered tree branches,
Drooping under the weight,
Icicles dangle all glittery and clear,
Looking as if they are made of crystal.

Snow covers all the land
With everything covered from trees to the ground,
Bare branches coated,
Fences as well,
Nothing escapes the wintry touch of
The snow and Jack Frost.

Snowflakes falling, dancing around,
Everything so delicate, not able to be touched,
Snow piles up all around the trees,
Everyone has got red noses and ears,
Winter days are so silent and cold.

Rebecca Weaver (11)
Courthouse Junior School

CLOUDBURST

A cloud is made of candyfloss,
That sits up in the sky
It's perfectly unreachable
For you or maybe I.

It sucks up all the rivers
And spits them out again
But we don't really think of this,
When it starts to rain.

Lisa Horbury (10)
Courthouse Junior School

What Is Spring?

Spring is . . .
The symbol of new life,
The glint in the rainbow.
Buds are ready to burst and sprout,
Vibrant colours shooting from every direction,
Hoping to come into view.
The sun is shining,
The birds are chirping - loud and clear
At the sign of the first dawn.

Spring really is . . .
Sitting inside on rainy days,
With grey clouds filling the sky;
Long days dragging on forever,
Waiting for that irresistible sun,
To break through.
Icy winds are blowing past me,
Reminding me of those cold winter days,
Or a dream in the deep of the night.

What is spring?

Sophie England (11)
Courthouse Junior School

THE BLITZ

Bombs are crashing, whining, falling
On a country deep in mourning.
Fires blaze and people cry
As screeching bombs go zooming by.

People flee and run for shelter,
While others scatter helter-skelter.
Bombs are raining through the air,
While sirens warn and fires flare.

The smell of burning's all around,
Confused people gather round.
Many come from under cover,
Silence now the night is over.

Danielle Zandi (11)
Courthouse Junior School

THE BLITZ

Crashing, splintering, all around,
Bits of glass are on the ground.
Flames are leaping really high,
Lighting up the dark, black sky.
Bombs are falling, crashing down,
Once there was a beautiful town,
Now there's rubble all around,
Piling high in one big mound.
I look around really scared,
Not that the Germans really cared,
Whether our town was deep in sorrow,
Or if we would be there tomorrow.

Sarah Jane Lee (11)
Courthouse Junior School

The Rhine

Fast flowing river in a V shaped valley,
Whispering, spluttering over the rocks,
Straight, fast and careless,
The trickle now becomes a stream,
Gushing down, further and further,
As it rumbles over the mini cliffs,
The jewelled fragments smash as it
Hits the thundering lagoon,
Snow-tipped for a second,
With bubbles bursting and floating away,
At sunset it never rests,
It keeps going through the night.

Night to day,
Child to adult,
It grows like you and me,
It gets wider, slower,
Totally different than before,
The grind, that it had done before,
Turns into an occasional crunch,
Suddenly it seems to go to sleep,
Restless from the day before,
As the boat goes up the Delta,
The Rhine turns ill from the boats' pollution,
At its old age near Rotterdam,
It trundles into the sea.

Andrew Bunyan & Harry Foster-Smith (11)
Courthouse Junior School

Spring Imagination

If you paint a picture in your mind,
The first things that you will find,
Are the lovely, bright colours of spring,
And the beautiful pattern on the starling's wing.

Daffodils, poppies almost everything,
These are the first signs of spring,
When the sun starts to come out,
This is the time when you can dance about.

Blossom has bloomed on the beautiful trees,
The flowers have begun to attract the bees,
They pick up pollen by mistake,
The nectar is what they had planned to take.

Hibernation is coming to an end,
All animals must find a friend,
It is now time for you to mate,
The cycle of life will not wait.

Francesca Cradduck (10)
Courthouse Junior School

The Rambling Rhine

From its sources the Hinter and Vorder
The Rhine starts to get slightly broader.
Foaming and frothing gushing downhill,
Past boulders and rocks, narrower still.
The river and hills in close parade,
Slowly the water starts to cascade.
Over and over the hills it flows
The flatter the land the slower it goes.

Nearer and nearer it winds to the sea,
Through Switzerland, Holland and Germany.
Carrying ships, barges and boats,
All laden with cargoes they steadily float.
Down to the ports and the towns by the sea,
Where the Rhine and her waters are finally free.

Camilla Bonfield (10)
Courthouse Junior School

THE RIVER RHINE

Icy, rapid, crashing water
Shifting, noisily down the mountain,
Over the polished rocks.
Transparent, frothy, splashing droplets
Filling the air with a sparkling scene.
As a sunbeam hits the water
A number of rainbow colours appear.
It makes a gurgling, rushing sound
Travelling for miles around.

As the Rhine is getting old,
And now passed through some towns,
The sparkling, springy stream we knew
Is polluted and murky, yellow and brown.
It meanders over the level ground
Hardly making a single sound.
Sadly reaches the sea,
Spilling forth the water
That's wanting to be free.

Julie Third (10)
Courthouse Junior School

The River's Route

The River Rhine starts off as a tiny trickle of water
Splashing, frothing and gushing over the rocks and boulders,
This very narrow stream twinkles in the sunlight like priceless
Diamonds
Swiftly making its way down the mountainside.

The river is rapidly slowing down,
But still by rocks it is getting churned around,
Wider now it keeps on getting
As it reaches the bottom of the mountains.

The river is lazily meandering along,
Becoming murkier and dirty and wider and slow,
The rocks and the boulders are fewer and fewer,
The sun reflecting on the water.

The water is nearly at the end of its journey,
Flowing very slowly, you can hardly see it move.
It has picked up lots of dirty pollution
Before it goes into the sea.

Sarah Blackmun (11)
Courthouse Junior School

The New Chick

Quietly the tapping starts,
Slowly it gets louder.
Cracks are spreading.
Suddenly the tapping stops.
The farmyard is in silence.

A small beak starts to emerge,
Then a tiny head.
The shell starts to shake
As the rest of the body appears.
Stumbling, tripping,
The chick makes its way
Across the run to the mother hen.
The whole farm holds its breath.
The air is hot and still.
A new life begins.

Gareth Lappin (10)
Courthouse Junior School

The Dashing Rhine

The river's calm and gentle flowing,
Gliding down the mountainside,
Then it crashes to the ground,
Fiercely bashing from rock to rock,
Soon it calms down getting slower,
Twisting, turning all around,
Vineyards, castles passing by,
Fascinated tourists gazing out,
Busy barges coming through,
Tourists rushing out of sight,
Dirty noisy people there,
Boats unloading cargo onto barges,
Slowly guiding past them all,
Coming to the river's end.

Clare Wilcox (11)
Courthouse Junior School

Diana, Diana

Everywhere,
Everyone,
Every city,
Every town,
Pictures and pictures
Click
Click
Click
All we wanted
More . . . more . . . more . . .
One day without warning
When we were wanting more,
The media and cameras
And us who wanted more . . .
Because of all our hunger
We lost
Our lovely British rose.

Caitlin Pickavance (10)
Emmbrook County Junior School

The Murderer

The murderer lives by himself
In a tall dark house
Full of stolen things
He's very tall and fat
His eyes stick out
His face frightens people
When he goes out killing you'd better stay in.

Tracey Stuka (8)
Hilltop First School

The Fading Star

Up in the sky a star appeared
It glowed like a lampshade alone in the dark.
It was yellow and gold with a glint of silver.
It stood there silently
It slowly went to sleep as the sun came out,
Then, the poor little star faded away.

Samantha Churchill (9)
Hilltop First School

Boys Like Me

Boys
like me
are sometimes
sexist, brave and bold
and sometimes dangerous.

Boys
like me
can be thin, fat
thin as a pin or
as fat as a cat.

Boys
like me
can be very lazy
and drive the teachers crazy.

Samuel Tudhope (9)
Hilltop First School

The New Boy

The new boy was a bully
He looked so fierce they cried
He had two big ears
A little nose
Two bulging eyes
Ten great big toes
His muscles grew and grew
Why he was a bully nobody knew.

Zoe Butler (9)
Hilltop First School

The Dragons Have Come To Town Again

The dragons have come to town again!
They come at night and give people a fright!
It's all a lark but the people don't know
But it's all to the park at night they go!

The dragons are furry and generally friendly,
But sometimes they're very nasty!

Thomas Pyke (8)
Hilltop First School

History And Me

I love history,
It is full of mystery.
Did Charles II have a son?
Who was James I?
Did he have a son?
Why did Lincoln die?
Who was the first English king or queen?
All these questions baffle me
That's why I like history.

Rachel Coenan (9)
Hilltop First School

The Maths Teacher

Our teacher has
A brain
But she works
With
Her cane
But she's a
Real pain
When
She hits you
Again and again.

Sam Quinlan (9)
Hilltop First School

The Sweets

Sweets are scrummy in my tummy
They bounce up and down in my
Scrummy scrummy tummy.
They are so sweet they squeak
In my scrummy scrummy tummy.

Samantha Lucas (6)
Holy Trinity CE Primary School

What Am I?

I can be brown, grey or white
A flowing mane and a big tail too
I have four strong legs
They eat hay
I have two ears
I am a horse!

Natasha Yellowlees (7)
Holy Trinity CE Primary School

Wintertime

In winter children love snow fights
They sometimes hit a car
They wrap up in woolly clothes to keep warm
On Christmas Eve, Father Christmas comes.

Matthew Aldridge (7)
Holy Trinity CE Primary School

FLUBBER

Flubber is good
Flubber is cool
Flubber is very bouncy and slimy.
Flubber is good at basketball
        and he scores every point.

Seth Miall (6)
Holy Trinity CE Primary School

TIGER

Tiger, tiger where shall I wander?
Upstairs, downstairs in my shower
Out in the garden, grass is green,
Tiger, tiger, can't be seen.

Francesca Kennett (6)
Holy Trinity CE Primary School

PIZZA

Pizza is my favourite food.
It gets me in a good mood.
I like it so much, I would eat it
today, tomorrow and the next day.
It would be a big one.
I would eat it so quickly that you wouldn't know
that I hadn't eaten it at all.

Tara Gooding (7)
Holy Trinity CE Primary School

Summer

The sun shines
you play football
you can relax
you can go swimming

Summer is fun
I wish it was summer all the time

I hope it is summer soon.

Nicholas Williams (6)
Holy Trinity CE Primary School

Football Club

Football Club
Football people playing
Football people scoring
Goal!
The goalkeeper was scared of the ball
Next goal was saved by the goalie,
It went straight to him.
The manager was pleased.

Joshua Thompson (6)
Holy Trinity CE Primary School

SLIMY

Slimy was very gooey
Slimy was fast
Slimy was fun
Slimy was bouncy
Slimy was silly
Slimy was an alien!

Daniel Headland (7)
Holy Trinity CE Primary School

THE DRAGON

The dragon breathes fire out of his massive nose.
He knocks the guards off their horses.
He runs till he flies.
He swoops down to land on hard ground.
He finds himself surrounded by guards.
He blows his fire till the land tumbles down.
All that remains of the hard land is
water.

Shivan Davis (7)
Holy Trinity CE Primary School

MY RABBIT

I have a white rabbit
He is called Rainbow.
He ate some cabbage.
I wonder what is next,
Some bread? No, some sweets.
Yes, they are nice and sweet.

Sasha Allgood (7)
Holy Trinity CE Primary School

The Bag Of Sweets

Mum brought in
a big bag of sweets.
Mum wasn't looking.
I took eleven sweets.
I felt a smack,
I took three more.
That was it
I ate them all.
I had to buy more sweets.

Edward A Clark (6)
Holy Trinity CE Primary School

Some Food Is Good For You

Some food is good for you!
Beans, peas, carrots,
Vegetables are good for you.
Sweets and chocolate aren't.
One day Suzy didn't know
    what to have for dinner.
Mum said 'Sizzling sausages.'
Suzy said 'Some sweets.'
Mum said 'No, afterwards.'

Natalia Wrigley (7)
Holy Trinity CE Primary School

SUMMER AT LAST!

In summer it is very hot.
You might catch a spot.
If you stay in the sun
You might get sunburnt.
In summer you can play tennis,
You can wear a T-shirt and shorts,
Sunglasses and a cap.
You can eat ice-cream and ice lollies.

Iona McKendrick (6)
Holy Trinity CE Primary School

TEDDY

My teddy has a scar
From where I did a test,
His rattle and his stuffing
Came out and made a mess.

My mummy told me off,
And sent me to my bed.
Teddy stared at me,
And smiled as he said:

'My tummy feels much better,
Though most of it's not there.'
His voice turned to a whisper,
'Although I'm still a bear!'

Ella Howell (10)
Robert Sandilands School

A FARAWAY LAND

I know a place a long way away,
Where no one must work, you can just play,
I know where a faraway land is,
It lies in the eastern part of the West Indies.
Five things I'd take with me are
My mum, my dad, my brother who's mad
And Tinker and Bob, my hamster and dog.
I know a place far far away,
Where no one must work, you can just play!
In the eastern part of the West Indies a long way away,
Is a special place I go to in May.
It's in May because everything is fresh.
The deer are out and that's why May is the best
To go to the *faraway land!*

Lizzie Isherwood (9)
St Andrew's School

BLADING

The wheels lovely, small but thick,
that's what I think of Nick.
Nick is a silly old fellow
and he always used to bellow.

When I do a power slide,
I end up on my backside.
I did a side surf
and I fell on some turf.

There is a foot-whiz
like popping lemonade fizz.
I did a grind,
But I became very blind.

Jamie Gough (10)
St Andrew's School

Day-Dreaming

I was sitting in my bedroom and
I was day-dreaming,
About dragons with their
Big mouths beaming.
They had big teeth and
They were so shiny and
Their little children,
They were so tiny.
I remember one,
She was three or four,
She didn't see a hole and
Fell under the floor.
I woke up with a start,
Then fell asleep,
Mum looked round the door
'Just taking a peep!'

Helena Stevenson (10)
St Piran's School

LONELINESS

Neglected and laughed at!
Names, colours, pictures, feelings, whizzing
Round my head, feeling your cheeks damp!
No, no, no!
When you're in bed, dreaming of Paradise
In the sky.
Snap out of your dreaming
To the lonely, dismal light!

Zoë Ellings (10)
St Piran's School

OLD WIDOW

A strange old widow walks down the street
Never says a word or anything
She walks down the street with a crooked old back
And a ragged old cloak and hat.

She's as old as a rotten egg and is rapidly ageing
But never seems to be changing
When she walks down that horrible street
Her feet seem to be shrivelling up!

Now she's gone and is never coming back
What's happened to her?
She's not come back, she must be dead
She's up in heaven in a cosy little bed!

Johan Olsson (9)
St Piran's School

My Mum

The ideal room for my mum,
Would be one right next to mine,
With a door going through,
So I could go in any time,
And she would sort out my problems.

If I didn't feel well,
I would go running through.
She'd give me some cream or gel,
And lots and lots of sympathy.

Inside she would have a bookcase,
With Agatha Christie books galore.
She would have a mini-fridge,
And only milk inside, for
One hundred cups of tea!

She would also need a kettle,
And a pot made out of gold metal,
And circular PG tea bags.

In there she'd need a piano,
To play 'Entertainer' and 'Für Elise',
And all along the top,
Would be fluffy toys, bears and bunnies.

And in her room there'd be no trace
Of jeans or dogs or cats,
Yet it's obvious that,
The ideal room for my mum,
Is a room right next to mine.

Lucy Foulkes (10)
St Piran's School

Mum

I see my mum,
Sitting on the sitting room chair
Listening to classical music
By Beethoven or Mozart.

She helps me with my homework
When I'm in a state
She is very clever
That's why she is great.

If I fell over in the playground
And then came home to her
Of course she would give me a plaster
And all the sympathy I need.

When I go into her room
I see her on her bed
But she isn't watching TV
She's reading a very long book instead.

Alix Coulter (10)
St Piran's School

The Summer Breeze

The summer breeze flows through my shiny hair.
The summer breeze flows through the willow trees.
The summer breeze is cold, cool and fresh,
And the summer breeze is kind of free.
The summer breeze suddenly disappears.

Aretha Roberts (11)
Sandy Lane Junior School

Rumble In The Jungle

If I lived in the jungle,
I would have so much more fun.
I would race the hippopotamus,
he would be so easy to outrun.
I would swing on the biggest trees,
with the funniest group of monkeys.
I would fly up high with the nicest birds,
while elephants are running in their herds.
I would have my drinks from the clearest river,
it would not be cold and make me shiver.
I would have my lunch from the ripest fruit,
instead of having hot warm soup.
The tiger would prowl in the hot warm light,
waiting for the snake to come out and fight.
But one of the nice things about all of this
is every day school would be dismissed.
So now you know why I am so bored
from opening the same old front door.

Chloe Collins (9)
Sandy Lane Junior School

Wet Wet Snow

In the winter long ago
walking through the deep wet snow.
There is snow on top of every wall
and every speck of snow the same,
and all our parents always know
where we go because of the footprints

in the snow!

Luke Metcalfe (8)
Sandy Lane Junior School

LISTEN!

Listen. Can you hear the sun rising in the sky?
Listen. Can you hear the dust screaming as it
gets sucked up the hoover?
Listen. Can you hear the toys speaking in your bedroom?
Listen. Can you hear the grass growing in the fields?
Listen. Can you hear the spider crawling across the floor?
Listen. Can you hear the stars flying through space?

Joe Hewitt (9)
Sandy Lane Junior School

LISTEN

Listen. Can you hear the pond weed grow?
Listen. Can you hear the ladybird flying?
Listen. Can you hear the ants crawling?
Listen. Can you hear the stars move away from Earth?
Listen. Can you hear the sun burn?
Listen. Can you hear the dust circle go round Saturn?
Listen. Can you hear Pluto being cold?
Listen. Can you hear the sun sweating?

Stefan Goniszewski (9)
Sandy Lane Junior School

Rivers

Rivers are cold,
Rivers are deep,
Rivers are fast, whizzing here and there,
Tossing and turning, gushing and splashing,
Rivers bending, curling, waving,
Meandering like a helter-skelter.

Ziggy Hughes (9)
Sandy Lane Junior School

Listen

The river is flowing downstream,
Listen, can you hear it scream?
As it goes down the waterfall,
Listen can you hear it call?

Now the river's spreading into a lake,
And the river says it's a piece of cake,
It is now on its way to the sea,
When it rains out of a cloud,
It falls to the ground,
And shouts out *'Wheeee!'*
It falls to the ground and waters the flowers,
It falls to the ground in showers and showers.

The river is flowing downstream,
Listen, can you hear it scream?

Joshua Beaven (9)
Sandy Lane Junior School

MONSTERS

I'm lying in my bed,
I'm feeling rather scared.
I hear a squeaky squeal,
Phew! It's only my hamster's wheel.
I saw something move,
It tipped over my hat,
Miaow! It's only my cat.
I really need to get to sleep now,
whether I like it or not
But I have to open the window,
it's getting rather hot.
I just saw something move over there
by my teddy bear.
Can't anybody else see the monster,
it's not fair!

Katie Lippett (11)
Sandy Lane Junior School

AUTUMN

Leaves falling in the wind
Animals hibernating in the winter
Acorns dropping out of the trees
Autumn leaves are falling
Helicopters float in the wind.

Daniel Cartledge (8)
Sandy Lane Junior School

THE RIVER

The day is dawning.
The sun is coming out.
Five fish swim past.
The river is flowing.
The shimmering sun up high.
I like the river.
It's lots of fun.
Six large frogs jumping about.
I think I like the trout.
The river is calm.
The day is nearly gone.
Now it's time to go.

Vicky Purcell (9)
Sandy Lane Junior School

THE LIFE AND DEATH OF A BUBBLE

The nacreous-looking bubbles wriggles out of the wand,
And drifts through the air hovering over children giggling.
The happy feeling seems to swim out shimmering across the room.
The glowing purple mixes with the fluorescent pink,
The yellow of the sun dims as it floats to the ground,
Swaying from side to side dodging the children's fingers.
It bounces on the ground showing its glassy transparent light.
It lies there thinking sad thoughts and slowly settles into the ground.
A spit of liquid and the bubble has gone.

Hannah Dorling (10)
Sandy Lane Junior School

DRY VERSUS WET

Wet whales swimming in the sea,
Dry ants climbing up the bark of a tree,
Wet children have a water fight,
Dry shells sitting on the seashore,
Wet water, wildly rushing in and out.

Michael Hammond (10)
Sandy Lane Junior School

WHAT CAN YOU HEAR?

What can you hear?
Cats miaowing
Dogs barking
Hamsters rustling
Are you listening?

What can you hear?
Fire burning
TV talking
People walking
Are you listening?

What can you hear?
Clock ticking
People kicking
People slipping
Are you listening?

What can you hear?
Teacher talking
Grass swaying
Are you listening?

Stephanie Reynolds (7)
Sandy Lane Junior School

Listening

Shhhh! I am listening
Shhhh! I am listening

I can hear
  A teacher shouting
  People playing
  A pencil writing
Are you listening?

I can hear
  Cars going
  Birds singing
  The wind blowing
Are you listening?

I can hear
  Teachers teaching
  Children reading
  Children playing
Are you listening?

Can you hear?

Martin Dixon (7)
Sandy Lane Junior School

Scorpion Haiku

Eight sturdy long legs
Walks in the African night
Eats with its sharp jaws.

Simon Baker (10)
Sandy Lane Junior School

Helping Others

Helping helping all around
Everybody willing to help
Love helping people now
People help other people
I help others
No one should be horrible
Girls are nice and boys are nice.

Jamie Soutar (7)
Sandy Lane Junior School

What Can You Hear?

What can you hear?
The siren,
Cars going past,
Dogs barking,
Are you listening?

What can you hear?
People talking,
People walking,
Teachers shouting,
Are you listening?

What can you hear?
Mum talking on the telephone,
Me eating,
Babies crying,
Are you listening?

Caroline Land (7)
Sandy Lane Junior School

In The Woods At Night

I slowly entered the dark wood,
The eerie wood was silent in the moonlight.
All that, but bats and slithery snakes
I kept a look-out for danger.
It started to pour with rain,
The rain was cold and heavy.
I was thoroughly drenched to the bone.
All my clothes stuck to me,
It was really uncomfortable.
I went deeper into the horrible wood,
The strange noises made the darkness terrifying.
The wind whistled around my hair,
Wet leaves brushed my face.
I tripped over a vine and fell in the mud.
Sharp branches prickled my legs.
A slug squelched under my foot,
Steamy and moist air.
Spiders crawled about in my clothes
I fell in a freezing lake.

Philip Woodgate (110)
Sandy Lane Junior School

Autumn

The wind waving
And the squirrels
Munch away
And the leaves
Are different colours
Brown, red and yellow.

Daniel Purcell (8)
Sandy Lane Junior School

Being a Child

Helping is to look after people.
Energy is when you are full of power.
Loving is to be kind to people.
Panicking is when you're scared.
Intelligence is when you're clever.
Nonsense is silly behaviour.
Good is when you're not naughty.

Obedient is doing what you are told.
Tantrum is when you cry.
Honest is when you tell the truth.
Enjoyment is when you're happy.
Running keeps a kid fit.
Selfish is when you don't share.

Matthew Bishop (8)
Sandy Lane Junior School

Autumn

Leaves falling on the ground
Animals always making a sound.
The wind is blowing, it's nearly snowing.
The bees are humming in the trees
Waiting for their honey bees.
Now the leaves are turning
Red, yellow, brown and orange.

Sadie Griffiths (7)
Sandy Lane Junior School

WINTER, WINTER

It is very cold.
My fingers are numb.
The lake is frozen and hard.
The snow is soft and cold.
I have a feeling that Jack Frost has been.
It is lonely and quiet.
The hill is covered in snow.
I see icicles on the trees.
The snow on the field is like a
                    thick white blanket.
Snowflakes are falling.
I get home and sit by the warm fire.
Tonight in bed, my nose is red.

Emma Lobar (9)
Sandy Lane Junior School

LISTEN

Listen. Can you hear the buds exploding as they come out?
Listen. Can you hear the tree roaring as it gets chopped down?
Listen. Can you hear the wolf thinking as it looks at its prey?
Listen. Can you hear the plants cry as the rain hits the petals?
Listen. Can you hear the trees chatting as they sway in the wind?

David Nicholls (8)
Sandy Lane Junior School

FIREWORKS

Traffic lights in the night.
Fireworks shooting in the night.
See red, yellow and green lights.
Rockets in the night.
I can hear soaring sounds.
Black cats in the sky.
I can see them
Getting hotter every time.
Onions in the oven.
I can hear *sizzling* sounds.

Matthew Wears (7)
Sandy Lane Junior School

THE CHIMNEY-SWEEP

My name is Tom the chimney-sweep,
Through tall sooty chimneys I creep.
The chimneys are so very steep,
From rooftop to rooftop, I leap,
Trying to earn my keep.
When I go home from being a chimney-sweep,
I'm so tired and hungry it makes me weep,
All I can do is fall into a heap!

Sam Dennis (9)
Sandy Lane Junior School

Can You Hear?

What can you hear?
The wind blowing
A plane is flying
And the traffic is loud
Are you listening?

What can you hear?
The trees blowing
And a car driving
And the telephone ringing
Are you listening?

What can you hear?
Spiders crawling on the floor
And a Concorde in the sky
And birds singing in the sky
Are you listening?

Danny Lalley (8)
Sandy Lane Junior School

Autumn

I can see squirrels
Leaves are falling
The wind is blowing, it's nearly snowing
Leaves are falling red and brown
The clouds are grey
We have to stay in our house for shelter.

Martin Aston (8)
Sandy Lane Junior School

AUTUMN

Brown autumn leaves,
Gently falling down.
Squirrels find some nuts
Then go in their tiny huts.
Different coloured leaves
Green, yellow, brown and red
Start falling on the leafy bed.
When the spring comes
The animals can get
Out of bed and be fed.
Windy weather blows a leaf
Like a feather
Squirrels get no bolder
When it gets colder
But get fluffy instead.

Alex Harvey-Brown (8)
Sandy Lane Junior School

FIREWORKS

Fireworks crackling in the sky
Catherine wheels going all about
Traffic lights turning red, yellow and green
Sausages sizzle on the barbecue
Fountains floating all about
Roman candle going *bang, bang!*

Amy Fairbridge (7)
Sandy Lane Junior School

RAIN

Rain is raining all around,
It falls on the green trees,
On cars and honey bees.
It falls on towns, farms and fields.
All through the winter it rained and rained
Pitter patter on the ground.
Wrap up warm,
Make a little sound
With your feet in the puddles.

Michaela Ambrose (7)
Sandy Lane Junior School

JUNGLE, JUNGLE

Monkeys swinging from tree to tree
having fun with a chimpanzee.
Watching tigers chasing their prey,
hyenas laughing all the way.
Thunder makes the animals scared,
now the animals are not prepared.
Lightning flashing and circling all around,
hits a tree and *kaboom!* It's down.
Now it's night and the owl is hooting,
the hunter is out and he is shooting.
Bats are squeaking in the cave,
so all the others better behave.
Now it's morning,
another day is dawning.

Graham Newell (9)
Sandy Lane Junior School

RAILWAY TRAINS

Inter-city goes fast.
Flying Scotsman flashes past.
Electric, diesel, steam.
To go on a train is a real dream.

Passengers waiting at the station.
Being late is a real sensation.
Stations have timetables
Engines run on overhead cables.

Stephen Wears (10)
Sandy Lane Junior School

ROLLER BLADING

When I wake up in the morning I just can't wait to
go out on my roller blades.
When it's time to get up I do everything so fast
and then I can put on my blades at last.
I go down to the sports centre, I get a lift from Gramps
He pulls up, I go on the ramps.
Jumping, grinding, spinning, turning,
I'm going so fast I can't hear my wheels churning.
I make a mistake, I'm beginning to fall
and I'm struggling with my back against the wall.
I go back home reading a book I borrowed . . .
Today was good, can't wait for tomorrow!

David Wilson (11)
Sandy Lane Junior School

Spring

Big petals, yellow leaves,
Blazing orange, gentle breeze,
Baby lambs, flowers too,
Rabbits, chicks, Easter eggs for you.
Sunflowers, tulips, crocuses as well,
Pansies brightly-coloured,
Then when the sky darkens the flowers become small,
They fall, close tightly, the colour disappears and fades away,
Night erases . . . away with the day.
The end of spring for another year,
          now a bright summer is here!

Ricarda Petrosino (10)
Sandy Lane Junior School

The First Time I . . .

The first time I went to the beach I thought
the sea was a piece of plastic,
The first time I touched the sea I shivered,
The first time I picked up seaweed I giggled softly,
The first time I swallowed sea water, I coughed
and spluttered out the salty water,
The first time I saw the sunset reflecting on
the sea I smiled happily.
The first time I had to go home I felt sad.

Louise Gardiner (11)
Sandy Lane Junior School

Trapped In A Bubble

Trapped in an iridescent bubble
Waiting to see a beautiful view.
People can see me.
I don't want people looking at me.
Up, up and away!
People are saying 'Who is that?'
                    and pointing at me.
I don't want this bubble to be transparent.
I want to get out of here.
The bubble starts to wobble.
I am scared that it will pop.
I am now in the sky forty metres up.
Now I can see everything.
It pops. *Ahhhhh!* I am falling,
What am I going to do?
The bubble saves me . . .
Pop!

Oliver Elmes (10)
Sandy Lane Junior School

Washing-Up

In the sink, the washing-up liquid goes,
Hot and cold water too,
We put in all the sticky pans,
And wash away the grease.

Blowing bubbles, rainbow colours,
As big as the sun in the sky,
Oh no! *Pop!*
It disappears before your very eyes.

Splashing each other as much as we dare,
Getting water everywhere,
But then we hear Dad come in,
And we think '*Oops!*'

Tidying up the mess we've made,
Is the worst of washing-up,
But there will be another time,
When we wash away all the grime.

Rosanna Lee (11)
Sandy Lane Junior School

EXAMS ARE TORTURE

Going to exams is torture.
Pencils or pens and paper waiting to be used.
Full of sweat as I turn on brain-power.
Shaking like mad.
I wish it was over.
It gets colder and colder
as I get deeper into the room.

I sit down and begin my work.
I begin to fall asleep.
I jump as my teacher knocks
on my shoulder.
As I get deeper into the work,
the adding gets easier.
It is the end of the first exam.
As I say 'Yes!' I get my jumper
to wipe the sweat off my face.

David John Collins (10)
Sandy Lane Junior School

THE CREATURE

Way way down in the deep lagoon,
a creature pops out at the sight of the moon.
It wades in the mud and there it lingers,
it has twelve toes and a hundred fingers.
It has one eye and three green feet,
at night it plays and by day it sleeps.
Instead of hair it has three red snakes,
it eats snail pie and spider cakes.
It has sharp claws and a ghastly roar,
it's inviting you to see its jaws!
In the morning when the birds sing their tune,
the creature returns to the deep, deep, lagoon!

Rachel Ward (11)
Sandy Lane Junior School

WASHING-UP

Washing-up can be fun,
Sparkling dishes for everyone.

Bubbles flying through the air,
Watch out, one is in your hair.

Ring the bell, ding, ding, ding!
There's a new washing-up liquid,
that smells like spring.

Alex Beaven (11)
Sandy Lane Junior School

The Life Of A Bubble

Flying out from a very high level,
Floating away seeing things you've never seen before,
Wobbling this way one second,
Catching all the views on my see-through skin,
All the iridescent colours swaying on my body,
I twist and turn floating high and low,
Don't know where to float to,
Don't know where to go,
Seeing all the scenes from the outside world,
I don't know when my life started,
Don't know when it will end,
Coming down to land, coming down, down, down,
Falling and drifting down to the ground . . .
Pop!
The life of the bubble is never ever seen again!

Shan Lee (11)
Sandy Lane Junior School

A River

A waterfall makes a long and thin river
which gives a shiver when the wind blows.
People sit and paddle their feet and
pack their picnics nice and neat.
Children decide to play beside the river
and watch it go by.
They listen to the sound of the river
crashing, smashing, bashing,
Goes the river mashing, bashing
Splat! Goes the river, swifting, drifting,
Shifting goes the river.

Vincenza Stevens (9)
Sandy Lane Junior School

THE VOYAGE

The green land disappears on the horizon.
The seagulls cry out,
over the creaking floorboards
of the deck.
The smell of salt overcomes the sea.
A distant rumble is heard far away.
The small drops of rain,
patter on the rotting wood of the ship.
The drops patter on the mussels,
that are clinging to the rocks like superglue.
Bloodsucking sharks look eagerly at the ship,
their huge mouths opening and shutting.
Suddenly a huge storm breaks out,
the sailors cry in terror.
The rain is drowning the ship with water,
they hit the ship like sharp icicles.
The waves hit the deck with a terrible force,
bolts of lightning flash down.
The rumbling's getting louder,
the sharks eating all the unfortunate sailors,
their mouths dripping with blood.
Then slowly the storm passes
The superglued mussels still cling on,
The boat is wrecked,
The sailors are dead.
The water is filled with blood,
and the sailors sink beneath the waves.
There is not a soul in sight.

Michael Entwistle (11)
Sandy Lane Junior School

The Life And Death Of A Bubble

Softly I blow through my wand,
A bubble is born.
It is iridescent and like a pearl,
I watch it as it floats through the atmosphere,
It seems to dance in the air,
Too happy to die,
It looks very light,
Then it lands on the floor,
It stays for a while,
But gives up the fight,
I think of it and start to smile,
Although I am sad,
Of the bubble I had grown quite fond,
In memory of it,
Once again, I blow through my wand.

Sarah De Caux (10)
Sandy Lane Junior School

Winter

Winter is cold,
The trees are old,
The leaves are brown,
Black leaves fall down,
The spiders are crawling,
The brown leaves are falling,
The bees are flying away.

Anthony Brooke (10)
Sandy Lane Junior School

WINTER

Frosted leaves all around
All you can hear are the trees aloud
Cobwebs glittery from the ground
You breathe warm and fog
Comes out all around.
We get a leaf and water falls down
I look up and a leaf comes down drippy wet
So I frown.
But it's wet and cold so
I want to get into the warm.

Harriet Hood (10)
Sandy Lane Junior School

SPRINGTIME

Spring is very lovely to watch the flowers grow
With pretty daffodils, buttercups, tulips and pansies.
The nice fresh air and the animals playing.
The soft ground and trees are bare.
The sky has got lots of clouds floating in it.
All the animals come out like birds in the sky
and foxes, squirrels and rabbits.
I love to watch the red and orange leaves rustling
on the ground as animals graze, not a sound.
The wind is blowing sweet fresh air.
I love spring.

Emma Purches (11)
Sandy Lane Junior School

SCIENCE

We did a science project
We had to try and find
The liquid that cleaned plates the best
And left no grease behind.

We blew a lot of bubbles
And we made a lot of mess
We got in lots of trouble
And we made our teacher stress.

I made my own commercial
I was a talking tap
I talked about the liquid
And then the liquid said a rap!

Coralie Gaskin (11)
Sandy Lane Junior School

FAT WHALE

There was a very fat whale,
gigantic and stale,
He was the size of the universe,
From the day he was born,
He was fat and high,
His head reached the sky,
His mother went frantic,
When he was born gigantic,
His friend was a shark,
He had a very big mark,
That went from its fin to his head.

Jerry Elkins (10)
Sandy Lane Junior School

The Life And Death Of The Bubble

The iridescence of the bubbles,
Glows in my face.
When I look into the bubbles I see myself.
In different colours I see my friends.
The eternity of the bubble has to end.
I picture myself as a bubble,
And so I imagine . . .
Oh I'm so looking forward to this,
My first flight.
First I'm liquid then breath pushes me,
It sets me free.
I'm in the air,
Floating in every crack, every corner.
Crash landing!
I'm coming lower and lower,
I am scared, cold and wet all over.
Bounce, bouncing, up and down,
Oh no!
Pop!
Oh how unfair, it must be dreadful.
Drastically falling down and down,
I'm happy - *being a human!*

David Garstang (10)
Sandy Lane Junior School

Lion Haiku

The beast of the night.
Roaring and chasing its prey.
The beast is the king.

Jack Seeman (10)
Sandy Lane Junior School

The Dark And Gloomy Hut

Wet and cold,
Muddy and brown,
in my boots I walked.
Along a path that I should go was a
hut with wooden walls,
I went inside to find nobody was there.

Inside this dark and gloomy hut were
four delightful bunks,
With one small desk and two great chairs
and wardrobes with no doors.

That night when I was in that dark
and gloomy hut,
There was a ginormous storm,
with rain that poured and wind that howled,
It was a great and fierce storm.

When the storm finally stopped,
I thought I had better check and see
what state my hut was in,
But when I looked around I saw a
figure in the room,
When I looked again I saw it was just a
friend!

Anna Russell-Smith (11)
Sandy Lane Junior School

SEED

I went for a ride yesterday
Guess what I saw upon the way?
I saw a deer, a fawn I should say
He picked me up and ran away.
I clung on as he ran around
Until he lay upon the ground.
I thought it would be safe to lie
In this good ground beneath the sky.
It rained and rained, it shone as well
And slowly I began to swell.
Into the ground I pushed my roots,
Up in the air sprang two little shoots
The years went by, I grew so high
My branches spread across the sky.
My fawn came back with antlers grown
Two fawns by him; his very own
This moment I've been waiting for
I cast my seeds upon the floor.

Tamsin Munday (10)
Sandy Lane Junior School

IN MY MIND

There is a world,
Deep in my mind,
Where dragons, like eagles,
Swoop, hunt and hide.

Elves make merry,
Drinking their wine,
Grapes plump and juicy,
Fresh from the vine.

In the mine,
A dwarf,
With his shovel
Digs for gold without any trouble.

This world is mine,
This world of thought,
And fantastic adventures,
Are just a thought away.

Robert Fabron (11)
Sandy Lane Junior School

The Raging River

The river was peaceful,
Glistening in the sunlight.
It began to rain,
The river started rippling.
The fish and frogs were going under
The raging water.
The river began pounding,
Rushing past the banks.
Soon you could hear roaring,
And crashing against the rocks.
Every second flowing down the river,
It got wider and wider.
Suddenly there was a loud crash,
The river exploded into the sea.

Robert Knight (9)
Sandy Lane Junior School

Bubble

Trapped in a bubble!

I'm trapped in a bubble,
Surrounded by air,
The bubble floating,
Soft and fair.

Pushing against the walls,
Trying to get out,
As it's twisting and turning,
It's wobbling about.

Out of a bubble!

You blow them away,
They're wishing to stay,
Give them a chance,
To bulge and dance.

Watch the bubbles float to the ground,
As they bounce,
And turn around.

Carina Keen (11)
Sandy Lane Junior School

The Lion

The lion is strong and stubborn.
He is king of all the land.
He has a mane around his neck,
Which makes him look so grand.
In the hot sweltering sun he sleeps
All day waiting patiently for his prey.

Joanna Martin (10)
Sandy Lane Junior School

Big

I've got a friend called Andrew
He is very tall
But if you compare him to me
I am very small.
I would like to be tall
As tall as can be
Maybe if you were very tall
You could see the sea.
Being tall is very very cool because
You see things at a distance
Far away you might even see *Italy!*

Stephen Emmerson (11)
Sandy Lane Junior School

The River

The river flows down and crashes against things.
It bashes against things as it goes past.
Everything it goes past, it nearly breaks.

Rivers are rough, rivers are strong, and sometimes
they can be calm.
It crashes against the sides and bashes against the rock.
Very fast it goes, whacking everything as it goes past.
Every day it bumps against something.
Rivers can sometimes be calm and smooth,

But other times . . .

Charlotte Knibbs (8)
Sandy Lane Junior School

The Petunia

In the garden of petunias,
there are birds and bees,
Among the weeds and the daisies,
we've got petunias and trees.

We've got the green, green pond,
with lots of fishes,
Daffodils and pansies,
mistletoe for kisses.

The sun shines brightly
and all the flowers loop
Because there's no rain,
they'll all droop!

Louise Lane (11)
Sandy Lane Junior School

My Little Sister

My little sister is very sweet
She is every sister's super treat
Although sometimes she can be bad
I do still love her but she makes me mad
She can also be quite demanding
But overall she is quite charming
I love her loads
I hope she knows
I love my little sister.

Lauren Hutchinson-Will (10)
Sandy Lane Junior School

My Baby Sister Ellie

Blue eyes, blonde hair
Rosy cheeks
Ellie has no cares,
She cries, she laughs, she's really perky
That's my baby sister, Ellie.
She's chubby and round
She bounces on the ground
That's my baby sister Ellie.
She crawls around and chases the cat
Then she falls down and goes *splat!*
A year ago she was in my mum's belly
Now I have my baby sister *Ellie.*

Kayleigh Holgate (9)
Sandy Lane Junior School

Grandpa

Sitting there smoking his pipe
Giving his eye a wipe.
I love him so
That grey hair has to go.
He was in the war
He still says he is sore.
When he sits on the floor
He is rather wrinkly
His face feels all tingly.

Gemma Dixon (10)
Sandy Lane Junior School

QUESTIONS

Questions, questions always questions.

Supergirl can fly,
Why can't I?

Flipper can swim,
But I'm not him.

Winnie the Pooh's a bear,
It's not fair.

Clouds make rain,
Why are they such a pain?

Pigs eat meat,
Why do I have wheat?

Why, why, why,
It's not fair.
Why don't I know the answers?

Laura Spurgeon (10)
Sandy Lane Junior School

MY FAMILY

My nanny is kind and friendly,
She buys me lots of things,
When I'm sad she comforts me,
When I'm ill she cuddles me.

My mum is very kind,
My mum is very friendly,
She does the washing and the cleaning,
When I'm sad she comforts me,
When I'm lonely she comforts me.

My dad is very caring,
He helps me get ready for my SATS,
Although he doesn't live with me,
I still love him.

They're all nice and caring,
They're all very friendly,
They're all kind and loving,
And I love them all.

Katie Johnson (11)
Sandy Lane Junior School

A Rainy Day

A rainy day is here,
A rainy day is here,
Crystal rain is falling in puddles.
A rainy day is here,
A rainy day is here,
Hear water splashing on the rooftop.
A rainy day is here,
A rainy day is here,
It's shiny on the ground, what a sight.
Wet watery weather,
Wet watery weather,
Droplets tapping on the window.
Wet watery weather,
Wet watery weather,
The mud is all soggy moist.
Wet watery weather,
Wet watery weather,
It's getting louder as it crashes down.

Craig Moore (9)
Sandy Lane Junior School

High Up In The Mountains

High up in the mountains
The water starts to flow
The water ripples
Through the mountain snow
The beaver starts to paddle
Through the river spring
High up in the trees
The bluebirds begin to sing
Peer through the bushes
A colourful rainbow stretches
From bank to bank
On and on the river rushes
Swiftly exploding into the sea.

Oliver Taylor (10)
Sandy Lane Junior School

Nappies

Nappies stink
Nappies smell
When you look at them
You feel unwell
But worst of all
When you're having your tea
Mum opens the nappy
Phew! Wiffy!

Alex Lowe (9)
Sandy Lane Junior School

Fireworks

Frightening, exciting, zooming and booming
Nowhere near a train whistle tooting
Making me jump, making me scared
Catherine wheels spinning
Sparklers sparkling
Whizzes and fizzes, crackles and bangs
Guy Fawkes on the bonfire
Fireworks going off, getting caught in the trees
That was the last of the firework display
Oh no! Here we go again!
Boom! Pop! Sizzle! Shock!
Now that was the end of the gunpowder plot.

Jenny White (10)
Sandy Lane Junior School

The River

The otter swimming to and fro
In the ice cold river
Eating fish all day long
River crashing on the rocks
Fish swimming up to the docks
Seagulls flying in the air
With ducks swimming everywhere
Then splash!
The water lapping on the rocks
Butterflies fluttering in the sky
Life goes on around the river.

Leigh Levey (9)
Sandy Lane Junior School

A Rainy Day

The dark clouds form,
The thunder begins.
A soft shower of clear crystals,
Falls from the heavens.
The faint tapping of gentle showers,
Begins.
The tiny droplets quench the flowers'
Thirst.
The land is moist, the land is fresh,
The dark clouds disappear,
The shower is over.

Jason Windmill (10)
Sandy Lane Junior School

All About Me

My name is Rebecca,
I like playing the flute.
I like going to Brownies.

My name is Rebecca,
I like singing,
I like going to ballet.

My name is Rebecca,
I like going to swimming.
But best of all,
Top of the hits,
I like my little sister.

Rebecca Comerford (9)
Sandy Lane Junior School

Sky Sports 1

Sky Sports 1
Is a bundle of fun
They've got all sports A to Z
They put them on there
Just for me
Sky Sports 1 is the best
Just wait and see
And that's the last you'll see of me.

Jamie Sweetzer (10)
Sandy Lane Junior School

The Wonderful River

A sparkling river flows by
Fish gleaming and twinkling bright
Otters splashing on the banks
Bulrushes swaying from side to side
Ducks' tails shivering
As their golden brown heads
Are dipped in the ice cold water
The river is roaring and crashing
Against the restraining banks
Now the wind is swiftly gliding
Over the crystal clear water
The wonderful river's life lives on
And beautiful things are happening.

Danielle Metcalfe (10)
Sandy Lane Junior School

BEACH

When I went to the beach
I went in the sea
My sister fell in
And tasted the water
And thought it was disgusting
We went to the fair
My sister caught her hair in candyfloss
We went home
With an ice-cream cone.

Daniel Bishop (10)
Sandy Lane Junior School

SALMON

The fish come in from the sea
The salmon come in herds
First they have to battle getting upstream
Only five out of ten make it
It's starting to rain, the water swirling and twirling
The salmon don't give up
They've come to the waterfall, it's time to do some jumping
They jump up and down trying to dodge the rocks
One hits a rock and falls back to the bottom
That's it, one more hard stream to battle out
Now they've finished but only one made it
But then he saw some more salmon
And asked them to be his friends.

Rick Curtis (10)
Sandy Lane Junior School

The Rain

All the creatures take cover,
Yet the frogs and worms come out.
All the mothers are complaining,
Because their washing is getting wet,
Children are splashing each other.
The car window wipers go,
Swish, swosh, swish, swosh,
That's the noise of the window wipers.

Chris Johnson (9)
Sandy Lane Junior School

The Crystal Clear Day

Continuous ripples forming crystal clear glitter puddles,
The rain falls like wet, soggy snowflakes,
Tapping gently on the window-pane,
The rain collapses to the wet ground,
Silence . . . no sound,
The rain splatters all around,
Gushing everywhere,
Everything glimmers.

The footsteps of men
Splashing through the puddles, it's still pouring down,
Drizzling, crashing, banging starts, tapping,
This is the sound of rain hitting the window-pane.

Sunita Suszka (10)
Sandy Lane Junior School

WINTER DAY

Winter day, winter day,
Snowflakes dropping from the trees.
Winter day, winter day,
Looking out of the shimmering window.
Winter day, winter day,
Seeing Jack Frost in the snow.
Winter day, winter day,
Freezing in the crunchy snow.
Winter day, winter day,
Slipping over on the ice.
Winter day, winter day,
Please never end.

Tyrone Elkins (9)
Sandy Lane Junior School

RAINY DAY

Water crashing down on windows,
Really hard,
Making puddles and squashy mud,
Clouds getting really heavy,
Raining hard,
Splashing and crashing everywhere,
Everywhere people getting really wet,
Running home from the rain,
It rains all day and all night,
People jumping in puddles and getting wet,
Now it has stopped.

James Cobain (10)
Sandy Lane Junior School

THE RAIN

The sky is grey,
The rain starts to fall,
Pitter, patter on the window-pane,
Droplets splashing on the glass,
Looking through the window,
I see people rushing to get home,
Children playing in the puddles,
Splashing, jumping in the water,
Doors are banging where mothers are collecting their washing,
Angry voices are heard,
The sky is breaking,
The clouds are going,
The sun starts to shine.

Robert Towell (10)
Sandy Lane Junior School

THE RIVER

Twisting and turning as the river flows,
Running to the sea,
Fish dashing, rain splashing.
Ducks swimming silently,
Flowing through the fields,
Past lots of trees.
Clashing and splashing on the rocks.
All the fish are now swimming, swirling and jumping.
Weeds are all wet and appearing soggy.
Everything is silent, not a word.
We are now near the sea.
We all made the journey to the sea.

Carla Mackay (9)
Sandy Lane Junior School

The Fish

The fish is fast as a bullet,
It swims and swims around the bends.
It's swirling and swimming,
Like a shark it will dart.
Twisting and turning,
The fish will twist,
It will start and then it will glow.
It will rip and then it will splash,
Turn and burn.
The fish will glitter at the bottom of the water,
And then the fish will float away to sea.

Mark Poole (10)
Sandy Lane Junior School

Alone

I'm a fish which is long,
I'm called an eel,
I swerve in the cold waters,
Side to side, gently and calmly, not a sound.
I grew up in the rivers of Europe,
But now I'm in the Sargasso sea.
The ripples move slowly along until they end.
I feel them along my smooth back, slivering.

I'm a fish which is long,
I'm called an eel,
Alone not a sound.

Sarah Taylor (10)
Sandy Lane Junior School

WATER NOISES

Dripping water, making ripples,
Drip, drop, splash, splosh.
Tapping on the windows making things moist,
Crystal drizzles wet and shiny,
Soggy mud, splat it goes.
Children splat in mud puddles,
Droplets dripping splash, splosh,
Swish, swoosh, side to side.
Ripples grow small to *big,*
Water dashing down the window-pane,
Wet water crystal-clear,
Mud squelching,
Crystal-clear water on the window.

Hannah Myers (9)
Sandy Lane Junior School

THE 4TH OF JULY

An annual holiday in the USA
Is the fourth of July, let's all shout hooray
In 1776 after a big mix
Two countries split and now it's a hit
It sure did pay
'Cause now we have Independence Day
Fireworks, laughing,
Red, white and blue,
Sparkling, shooting, swirling too,
That's what fireworks do.

Jacqui Ross (10)
Sandy Lane Junior School

Life In Tudor Towns

Tudor towns were busy,
But not so busy at night,
Dirty, smelly, filthy water was flung from the windows,
People got attacked at night,
If they did they would get a fright.

Horse and carts driven by men,
On the back is a big fat hen,
Fat, drunk men out at night,
They are probably the people who give you a fright.

Nicky Winsper (10)
Sandy Lane Junior School

Rain

Splashing rain against the ground,
Just like crystals coming down,
I see some puddles,
Ripples in watery water,
Tapping loud outside,
But soft tapping inside.

Shiny ripples,
Going out,
Into circles,
Crystal clear,
Soggy water is coming down,
Drizzling outside,
Now the time has come,
I go outside and splash about in the puddles.

Sammy-Jo Weston (10)
Sandy Lane Junior School

DRIP, DROP

The shiny droplets on soggy ground,
While the crystal clear rain is tapping all around.
Drip, drop, drip, drop,
There are ripples on the puddles,
As the crashing rain comes splashing down,
Drip, drop, drip, drop.
The watery mud goes splash, splash,
As the rain comes tumbling down,
Drip, drop, drip, drop.
See the ground get soggy,
As the crystal droplets seep through its soil,
Drip, drop, drip, drop.
The shiny crystal droplets have made the whole world wet,
But still they come crashing and splashing on the grit,
Drip, drop, drip, drop.
The moist ground is drying,
The shiny crystal droplets have gone, gone, gone . . .

Charlotte Lindsay-Kipp (10)
Sandy Lane Junior School

JUNGLE SNAKE

Snake in a jungle, got to beware.
They might come out and bite you.
Snake's in the jungle going up and down a tree.
Looking for its prey.
People say that they battled with a snake, but is it true?
Jungle, got to beware.

Charlotte Dixon (9)
Sandy Lane Junior School

My Life As A Fish

Splashing and crashing in the river,
The wet cold blue life is for me,
I dash down the river,
Frogs jumping in the water,
It's only the wet cold blue life for me.
With seaweed and shells at the bottom,
You should wonder why I live in the cold blue river.
I'm roaring and crashing but the fisherman is coming,
I'm going to hide.
The fisherman has caught me in his net,
I no longer live in the wet cold blue river.

Lee Poole (10)
Sandy Lane Junior School

A Rainy Day

Crystal clear droplets start to tap on the window,
The thunder starts to rattle and fall to the ground,
The ground is getting moist,
The mud starts to get soggy,
Some puddles appear with eternal ripples.
The water starts to crash to the ground,
The thunder bangs again,
Suddenly it all stops,
Rain drips from the pipes and the rain has stopped.

William Croxford (9)
Sandy Lane Junior School

THE BODY POEM

My feet walk,
My hands write,
My heart beats,
So I can live my life away,
My body, my body.

My feet skip,
My hands can throw,
My heart beats,
So I can live on my own,
My body, my body.

My feet leap,
My hands can feel,
My heart beats,
We live because our heart beats,
My body, my body.

Emma Dixon (9)
Sandy Lane Junior School

LISTEN

Listen, can you hear the ants trot up the tree?
Listen, can you hear the stars chatting to each other in space?
Listen, can you hear the ladybird flap its wings as it flies away
from the window-ledge?
Listen, can you hear palm trees talking to each other?
Listen, can you hear the clouds moving from side to side in the sky?
Listen, can you hear the candyfloss being squashed in someone's
mouth?

Jodie Giles (8)
Sandy Lane Junior School

ALLITERATION POEM

One white whale waiting for food,
Two tiny tadpoles twisting and turning,
Three thumping thieves fighting for food,
Four friendly ferrets floating forwards fast,
Five ferocious folks fishing for fish,
Six silent seals slithering,
Seven slithering snakes talking to seals,
Eight elephants eating eels,
Nine naughty knives knitting,
Ten tigers take Tikka.

Emily Bryant (10)
Sandy Lane Junior School

WHAT IF?

What if there is a spider in my bed?
What if I am late for school?
What if my mum and dad break up?
What if the pool is shut?
What if I eat poison?
What if the postman gets eaten?
What if I am a ghost?
What if I am a witch?
What if I go to school in my nightdress?
What if I am a dumb at school?

Lindsay Windmill (8)
Sandy Lane Junior School

THE SOUNDS OF THE RIVER

Crashing, bashing, slashing,
That's the sound of the river.
Whirling, twirling, swirling,
That's the sound of the river.
Swifting, drifting, sifting,
That's the sound of the river.
Cracking, whacking, smacking,
They're all the sounds of the river.

Nicola Street (9)
Sandy Lane Junior School

WATERFALL

The river roaring, smashing against the rocks
It suddenly comes down an enormous waterfall!
Birds singing in the sky
The tree swishing in the wind
The wind whooshing, pushing
It makes the river go on and on
Fish swimming, frogs jumping off the rocks
The waterfall makes a splash!
The ripples go down the stream
Here we go again
The water hog plunged over the edge
And continues down the stream.

Hayley Blackall (10)
Sandy Lane Junior School

THE JUNGLE

The jungle is full of animals,
the tiger, eagle and snake!
The cobra spits poison.
The rattlesnake shakes.
The eagle feeds on its prey.

But the tiger hides and
when it's in range, it pounces . . .

The king cobra is tall,
about six foot high,
the mongoose strikes and
eats him at night!
Pumas are black and
blend in at night.
Flying squirrels are
so clever and light.
When he jumps
out a tree, he glides
like a feather.

Daniel Boyles (8)
Sandy Lane Junior School

SNOWFLAKES

Falling softly from the sky like pieces of fluff so white.
Shimmering, sparkling pieces of fluffy, shining light.
From the clouds, floating, drifting gently to the ground,
As they twirl, as they shine, silence is the only sound.

Frosty trees with glitter icicles, sparkly trees, dripping trees,
Everywhere green plants are disappearing, the land starts to freeze,
As the snow keeps on falling, snowballs pile up to throw.
Winter is here, crystal trees, freezing fingers and glowing white snow!

Rebecca Hawkes (10)
Sandy Lane Junior School

FIREWORKS

Fireworks
Pop and crack
Zoom and whiz
Bang and whoosh
They all go up in
One, two, three!
Fireworks
Are so exciting
They make me
Pop out of my skin!
S c r e e c h
Go the fireworks
In the sky
Fireworks glitter
Like the sky is falling
Fireworks may not look
Dangerous
But they are!
I like them so much
I would like to see them
Every day!

Christopher Merton (8)
Sandy Lane Junior School

THE CHIMNEY SWEEP

I am up before the sun,
there is no time for fun.
I am so thin and small,
I climb chimneys so tall.
I climb and climb and must not stop,
until my head sticks out the top.
At the end of the day with so little pay,
my dinner is bread and I have no proper bed.

Danny Bungay (8)
Sandy Lane Junior School

JUNGLE POEM

I walk through the jungle and what do I see?
A monkey swinging from tree to tree.
Oh! What fun that must be.
I walk along a bumpy path and what a surprise, I see a giraffe.
The rhino's rumply skin is too big for him to fit in.
The sun beats.
Oh! The sweltering heat.
Dripping water falls from the hot, tropical sky.
Chattering monkeys, twittering birds,
The tiger prowls among the long, green grass, watching its prey.

Emily Hanbury (9)
Sandy Lane Junior School

About An Autumn Morning

The acorns falling out of their shells
The spiders spinning silky webs
The beetle underneath a leaf
These are the things you'll find on an autumn day
The grass all jewelled with dew
The leaves all wilting off the trees
The leaves all on the ground covered in frost
These are the things you'll find on an autumn day
The leaves are falling, each one dancing
Plants are frosty white and glittery
These are the things you'll find on an autumn day
Crunchy leaves on the ground
Icy and jewelled with the frost
Wet and melting, spiky leaves
Shining in the sun
These are the things you'll find on an autumn day.

Katherine Williams (11)
Sandy Lane Junior School

What If?

What if ET jumps out of my TV?
What if I see a ghost in my bedroom?
What if Edward Scissorhands jumps in my window?
What if there is an alien in my bed?

Jay Lee Dallas (8)
Sandy Lane Junior School

FIREWORKS

Fireworks go *pop*
Fireworks are dangerous
Fireworks are light
And glittery
I like fireworks
Fireworks are colourful
Fireworks go zoom
Fireworks are fun
Guy Fawkes died
On fireworks day.

Limara Banks (7)
Sandy Lane Junior School

PEACEFUL WORLD

Fish shimmering, ice cold in the water.
Twinkling stream, running and roaring.
Insects swimming on the surface.
Birds swooping down for fish.
Wind rushing through the river.
The wind whooshing through my hair.
Sparkling leaves floating on the surface.
The water sparkling in the sunshine.
Frogs laying eggs in large bundles.
Butterflies float overhead.
All is peaceful.

Zoe Booton (9)
Sandy Lane Junior School

WHAT DOES A RIVER DO?

The river is silent wherever it goes,
it is smooth as it runs along.

At night you can see the sky as clear as a picture,
it stays still, calm, lonely and very peaceful.

When the sun rises at the crack of dawn,
the river water sparkles as it goes along.

Next to the river bank lies a river
that floats down under the bridge.
Maybe one day it will become part
of the big, blue, wet sea.

Christen Gaskin (9)
Sandy Lane Junior School

THE THINGS I WILL MISS

I will never be allowed to see my friends
playing in the snow and jumping about.
Thunder crashing, rain banging.
I would miss the ducks quacking.
When the world ends, the sun will never shine,
the thunder will never flash.
I would miss the sheep getting put away
and my dog running away.
I would miss Concorde and planes racing across the sky.
But now everybody is saying goodbye.
I would miss seeing the boat sailing to sunset.
I love to hear the robins singing.
Now the world's over we won't have any sunshine.

Scott Wilson (9)
Sandy Lane Junior School

THE RIVER

Splashing, bashing, crashing, dashing,
The river is very angry.
Lonely, peaceful, silent, still,
The river is very calm.

Herring, haddock, salmon, pike,
And other fish swim,
Along the river, calm or angry,
They must be having fun.

Waving, weaving through big rocks,
Through wide and narrow valleys,
And suddenly as it reaches the edge,
Down,
    Down,
        Down . . .

It reached the waterfall at last.

Victoria Fabron (8)
Sandy Lane Junior School

LISTENING

Can you hear
    Birds singing
    Teachers calling
    Did you hear the tree rustling?
Listen, please listen

Can you hear
    Cars coming
    Someone coughing
    Birds still singing?
Listen, please listen

Can you hear
Children talking
A car starting up
Someone sneezing?
Listen, please listen

Can you hear
Children's footsteps
A rubber rubbing out a page
Can you hear a clock ticking
And a pencil drawing?
Listen, please listen.

Emily Hawkes (8)
Sandy Lane Junior School

My Shoe

I designed a shoe
Which has loads and loads of gadgets
I wish my shoe was real.

My shoe has
A rocket at the back to fly through the air
Three parachutes to land safely on the ground
A water pistol to squirt other people
A control pad to control the shoe
A horn to warn people that I'm coming
A windmill to lift me off the ground
An aerial to pick up the signal from the control pad.

I designed a shoe
Which has loads and loads of gadgets
I wish my shoe was real.

Daniel-Thomas Horscroft (7)
Sandy Lane Junior School

In The Jungle

In the jungle quiet.
Not a sound.
Insects crawling on the ground.
I am spotted and very fast.
If you meet me you're sure not to last.
I am quick and very small.
Quick as a leopard, a leopard I am.
I hide out of sight, I come out at night.
If you find me if you dare, I'll be hiding in my lair.

Hannah Edwards (9)
Sandy Lane Junior School

My Bike

I like going
On my bike
I like
Doing wheelies
They're
Dangerous
And great fun!
I like
Spinning around
On my front wheels
I like going
On my bike
Up the park
Because it's quite steep
I like going
On my bike.

Sean Rich (7)
Sandy Lane Junior School

Autumn

Autumn is cold and wet
Autumn is when the trees lose their leaves
Autumn is slippery and foggy
Autumn is when squirrels collect nuts
Autumn is when the leaves turn colours
Autumn is when it is damp at night
Autumn is when you have colds
Autumn is when you slip
Autumn is soggy.

Lorinda Robert (7)
Sandy Lane Junior School

What If?

What if I die?
What if I turn into an alien?
What if somebody kidnapped me?
What if the floor ate me?
What if the school falls down?
What if I have kids and they smoke?
What if I have dreams and a monster comes into my bedroom and gobbles me up and then goes into my mum and dad's bedroom and gobbles them up?
What if?

Harry Skinner (8)
Sandy Lane Junior School

Autumn

Autumn is cold mornings
Autumn is early dark nights
Autumn is plants dying off
Autumn is squirrels collecting nuts
Autumn is birds searching for berries
Autumn is people wearing warm clothes
Autumn is fish swimming to the bottom of the ocean
Autumn is leaves crowding around my feet
Autumn is all different colours
Autumn is my dad's birthday.

Daniel Viccars (8)
Sandy Lane Junior School

Fireworks

Fireworks go pop
Fireworks are dangerous
Fireworks go zoom
Fireworks are exciting
Fireworks are loud
And
Fireworks glitter

Fireworks are red, pink, yellow and blue
Fireworks go up in the sky
Catherine wheels go round
And
I like fireworks!

Kelly Faulkner (7)
Sandy Lane Junior School

What If?

What if I get bullied?
What if I get my ears pierced?
What if I break a glass?
What if the teacher shouts at me?
What if I don't like the head teacher?
What if my cat bites me?
What if my cat dies?
What if Mr Ayscough leaves the school?
What if my mummy and daddy die?
What if Kelly breaks up with me?

Zoe Hammond (7)
Sandy Lane Junior School

Myself

This is a poem about
Me!
I like playing around
And being silly
I like sweets a lot
My favourite is chocolate
And I like football
I like going out
And seeing my grandad and grandma
And at bedtime
I like staying up on Saturday and Sunday nights.
So this was a poem about
Me!

Phillip Little (8)
Sandy Lane Junior School

LISTENING

Can you hear
Rubbers rubbing
Cases shutting
Pens falling
Are you listening?

Can you hear
Children playing
And the whistle blowing
And chairs creaking
Are you listening?

Can you hear
Pencils drawing
A car starting
And what about
A motor bike
Rumbling?
Are you listening?

Sam Sweetzer (8)
Sandy Lane Junior School

LISTEN

Listen, can you hear?
The leaves screaming as they tumble down to the ground,
The dust shout as it gets sucked up the hoover,
And can you hear the explosion of a bulb when a flower grows?

Listen, can you hear?
The moth's foot stamp on the grass when it walks,
The sun yawn when it wakes up,
And can you hear the mist walking across the fields?

Listen, can you hear?
The eggshell cracking as the baby bird is born,
The sky moan when the thunder gives it a headache,
And can you hear the scissors laugh when something is cut?
If you can't, listen, just listen.

Toni Fidler (8)
Sandy Lane Junior School

FIREWORKS

Fireworks fizzle in the air
They are very colourful
Red, yellow, blue, purple
And other colours too!
Tonight is Firework Night
Off starts the Catherine wheel
Here come the sparklers
Sssssssss
Fireworks are dangerous
Children shouldn't *play* with fireworks
Zoom
Whiz
Pop
Bang
Go the fireworks
They sparkle and are like glitter in the sky
One, two, three, go, into the air
Off they go!

Stewart Tibby (7)
Sandy Lane Junior School

What If?

What if a spider came into my bed?
What if I get blue cheeks?
What if I die?
What if there is a fire and I can't wake my family?
What if my toys come to life?
What if I fall out of the window?
What if I fall asleep in class?
What if I do bad work at school?
What if I turn into a monster?
What if I get an informal warning?

Jessica Johnson (8)
Sandy Lane Junior School

Little Hamster

Little hamster came to my house,
Little hamster size of a mouse,
Little hamster plays on his wheel,
Goes on and on until he feels ill,
Poor little hamster crawls to his bed,
With a very, very bad ache in his head,
After his sleep, he felt much better,
He had a drink and his whiskers got wetter,
I love my little hamster.

Matthew Blackall (9)
Sandy Lane Junior School

Monsoon

Grey clouds puffing up,
here the rain's falling,
see the ripples on the holy river,
people giving presents to the holy river.

Monkeys swing on green vines,
crocodiles snapping their jaws,
fishes' scales glinting,
birds singing their ringing songs,
splat!
Monkeys throwing bananas,
running, running.

Through the dark forest,
I trip, I stumble,
running, running,
to my home,
home at last.

Hudson Holt (8)
Sandy Lane Junior School

In The Jungle

When you go to the jungle,
it is dark, creepy and wild.
The tigers roar,
the waterfalls crash against the rocks.
The monkeys jump from tree to tree,
the snake's travelling across the muddy floor
slithering silently.
The jungle is dark and creepy.

Jake Roberts (8)
Sandy Lane Junior School

Ganges Poem

The animals wake up to wash in the river.
The crocodiles wake up for their morning meal.
People bring gifts to the holy river Ganges.
But a crocodile spots them and swims to the people.

A quick loud noise, flashes in the sky, it is the monsoon.
Everybody shelters in their home until the rain stops.
The rain pats against the soft earth.
The animals find a safe place to stay.

The monsoon stops leaving a flooded landscape.
People climb out to find a boat to look for food.
Crocodiles look for fish to eat by themselves.
The fish try to escape but they get eaten.

The monsoon flood starts to disappear.
The boats start sinking.
The houses grow higher.
The fish die.

Mark Baker (9)
Sandy Lane Junior School

My Little Brother

My little brother, he screams and shouts all day.
My little brother plays and plays and plays.
My little brother, he does not go to school.
My little brother, sometimes he's an absolute fool.
My little brother, he sucks his dummy
And after all he loves his mummy.

Pasquale Small (8)
Sandy Lane Junior School

Space

Space is dark,
Space is glittery,
Space has no gravity,
Space has a lot of brightness,
Space has a giant sun,
Space has many planets,
Space has a satellite,
5, 4, 3, 2, 1 blast off.

Bradley Cronin (8)
Sandy Lane Junior School

Space Rocket

Flying, flying
in a rocket
what do I see?
A planet far away from the Earth,
it's very small.
A flash of light comes in my direction,
then total darkness.
Flying, flying
in a saucer,
I go in a different direction
and go to a big planet
with a ring around
and red fluffy clouds.
The saucer bangs against the ground.

Jonathan Williams (9)
Sandy Lane Junior School

GOLDFISH!

G oldfish are slippery,
O range and slippery,
L ovely and gold,
D ucking and diving,
F loundering around.
I n the swirling water,
S o small is their brain,
H ow they struggle and strain,
to remember something,
four seconds ago.

Robert Swain (8)
Sandy Lane Junior School

A COLD DAY

Cold, cold, it's a very cold day.
Children shivering, children going skiing.
Going to school in the car.
Children laughing, ha, ha, ha.
Inside it is very warm.
Mums and dads curling up in bed.
Children having nice hot drinks.
The leaves falling off the trees.
Children's faces and noses going red.
Children having snow fights.
What a windy day.
It is a miserable day.
During the night Jack Frost came and put ice on the cars.
Children making snowmen.
Ouch, someone hit me with a snowball.

Siobhan Burns (9)
Sandy Lane Junior School

AIR

Wind blowing all around you,
You can feel it but you can't see it.

Refreshing to welcome, smooth and calm,
Ghostly.
Air all around the earth.

Francessca Nightingale (9)
Shaw-cum-Donnington CE Primary School

FIRE

Fire, fire
Spreading, burning
Fire, fire
Scolding, angry
Transforming rainforest to ashes.

Man made hell
Rainforest nightmare
Spreading, burning
Scolding, angry.

Ella Stirmey (10)
Shaw-cum-Donnington CE Primary School

Fire

Fire looks like a mixed-up rainbow,
It smells like a big stick of charcoal.
Fire sounds like a child screaming,
And feels like a knife stabbing into you.
Fire tastes like a hot chilli sauce,
It swallows up all in its path.

Catherine White (10)
Shaw-cum-Donnington CE Primary School

The Hippopotamus

The hippopotamus lay down on its back,
And rested in the evening sun.
The hippopotamus went to bed,
And sound asleep it went.

The hippopotamus woke and started to move,
The hippopotamus opened its mouth and yawned.
The hippopotamus went to its breakfast,
And gobbled it up.

The hippopotamus went to its gym class,
Then had a very big lunch.
The hippopotamus had a very big swim,
Until the evening arrived.

That's my hippopotamus swimming in my pool,
That's my hippopotamus gobbling down ten of my boules
It's my hippopotamus,
Whose did you think it was?

James Ramsay (11)
Silchester House School

SPRING

The plants rise
Out of the ground,
Their flowers burst
Like fireworks.

The lambs walk
For the first time,
Their tails wagging
Happy it's spring.

The birds sing
A joyful song
Building their nests
In harmony.

Jonathan Naylor (11)
Silchester House School

THE ELEPHANT

There once was an elephant,
In the zoo,
I stared at it,
It ran away.
I fed it until all the bananas were gone.
It came nearer and did a big trumpet
And it meant to say,
'Have you got any more bananas?'

Daniel Wong (10)
Silchester House School

The Elephant

The elephant is kind and strong,
The elephant is a lovely animal,
And I think it's wrong for us
To kill them for tusks.

The elephant is kind and strong,
A gentle giant with trunk so long,
Its kind face with its large grey ears,
King of his land, he has no fears.

The elephant is kind and strong,
He leads his family and lives so long,
He's true and clever, wild and free,
A beautiful animal he'll always be.

Joanna Rhodes (10)
Silchester House School

The Dolphin

A cross the deep clear water
N earing closer to the caves
I see a large blue dolphin
M oving swiftly through the waves
A nd as I sit here watching up the soft warm sand
L oving every moment of the wonders in this land.

Emily Macura (9)
Silchester House School

POLLUTION

Acid rain falls
No birds in the sky
Nothing to be heard
No fish in the lake
The trees stand bare
No sign of buds
The lake is full of rubbish
There's a layer of oil on top
Factories don't stop giving out
Fumes which kill the countryside.

Neil Davidson (9)
Silchester House School

POLLUTION

Pollution, pollution is
A very bad thing,
Other people smoking,
Is very annoying.
Petrol fumes from cars
Are smelling

A beach covered in oil
Makes sand black like soil
I wish all this would stop
It endangers the earth a lot.

Rebecca Hawes (10)
Silchester House School

THE WITCH'S CAT

The witch's cat is black and white,
With long sharp teeth,
And long sharp claws,
It has a long, long tail,
And big round eyes.

He helps the witch with all her spells,
He stirs the cauldron round and round,
It's the witch's cat,
Look! There's the witch. Look!
I can see her, can you?

The witch's hair is red and green,
She has a sharp pointed chin,
And a tall black hat,
She has a long, long stick,
And she rides it with her cat.

Christine Taylor (7)
Silchester House School

BADGER WATCHING

Settling down,
Getting comfy,
Looking around,
Just waiting.

Hopes high,
Getting dark,
Pins and needles,
Still looking.

Looking hard,
Stars appearing,
Owls hooting,
Still looking.

Getting restless,
Hopes going,
Getting bored,
Hopes now gone.

Tomas Kinmonth (11)
Silchester House School

What Have We Done To Our Earth?

The fields are full of corn,
The sky's a sweet, clear blue.
More baby lambs are born.
The clear sea that we knew.

The ponds are mucky grey,
They seem to match the sky!
Grass is turning into hay,
Dark clouds are floating by.

The paths are not clean and aren't healthy.
There's pollution in the air,
The countryside used to be wealthy,
But now there's rubbish everywhere.

The air is as black and black can be,
Dark water covers the ground.
Not a bird in any tree,
No people, not a sound.

Victoria Mizon (10)
Silchester House School

POLLUTION

Don't pollute it's bad for the earth.
You ruin the trees,
You ruin the seas.
We are lucky to have
Our trees, our grass, our sky and our seas.

There are many ways to pollute the earth.
To drop litter in the rivers,
To ruin the grass.
It's as dry as grasshoppers
Who jump and hop past.

The fumes from factories,
Travel to Scandinavia.
They turn into acid rain
Which kills all the trees.

We must be more responsible,
We shouldn't pollute - it's bad.
We can help the grass, the trees, the sky and the seas
And then you will be glad.

Carly Hazelton (10)
Silchester House School

THE CAT

He lurks on the garden,
He lurks in the sun
He lurks on the hill
He's now on the run.

He stole some fish
Away he ran,
Back to his owner
To put in the pan!

His owner was shocked
That the cat got out,
And so the next day
The cat got sprouts.

That's the story of the cat
His name is Billy
Now he's very old,
it's very, very silly!

Natalie Jessica Fulker (10)
Silchester House School

Pollution

Pollution is bad for us,
We breathe it in all day.
It's caused by the cars and chimneys,
That pollute us every day.

Pollution in the water, is killing all the fish,
Because chemicals are spreading in the river,
Which means fish are dying
Day by day.

So please help by recycling,
Be careful what you do with waste.
Try not to cause pollution,
We must protect nature.

Christine Ramsay (9)
Silchester House School

POLLUTION, POLLUTION IS THERE A SOLUTION? IS THERE, IS THERE?

Stop factories belching
Their fumes in the air,
And the beaches
All covered in oil.
Don't stop, to spoil the countryside
Or to spread more oil.

Think of the animals,
Don't poison the flowers
Or chase the birds and bees
Think of the trees that are
Dying of pain, all by the acid rain

There is a solution
For all the pollution,
Just don't throw your rubbish away.
You can have fun, when the pollution is done,
Just behave.

So think of the solutions for all the pollution
And don't throw your rubbish away!

Pollution, pollution, is there a solution?
To keep all the rubbish away?

Holly Pink (9)
Silchester House School

Flowers

Flowers spring from the ground
Lilacs, roses, tulips. Oh what's that?
Look, pink, purple, yellow and red
Buds coming out from the trees
Each little and big flower coming out
Robins, crows, birds in the air
Looking down at the flowers everywhere.

Karla Flower (9)
Silchester House School

Slough

Slough is a very industrialised place
The town is quite a big place
It has different kinds of race
It is quite a dangerous place.

Slough is the best place
For all kinds of race
I like going there
It's my best place.

Kirun Dhesi (10)
Silchester House School

Look At That Person Mummy!

Look at that person Mummy,
Throwing that bottle over the hedge.

Look at that person Mummy,
Throwing that crisp packet into the trees.

Look at that person Mummy,
Hiding that box in the bushes.

'Oh just shut up . . .
And don't you *dare* drop those sweet papers!'

Mummy I would never do anything like that!
Ooops!

Christopher Sainsbury (9)
Silchester House School

Up, Up & Away

One day in the boiling sun.
I was carried to a big space shuttle.
They put me in a suit
and I went into the dark black upper atmosphere
I saw the Milky Way and Mars
What an adventure.

Richard Kindred (9)
Stoke Poges School

SPACE COMPUTER

So there I was back in the study,
I couldn't go out it was way too muddy,
I played on my computer game 5-4-3-2-1 and off I went into the
space world.
It was ever so bright and I would not like to tell you the height it was,
It was a wonderful sight,
I put on my space clothes and off I went landing.
I opened my eyes. I must be asleep.
But I knew I wasn't dreaming. I saw the Space Girls.
They took me into a rocket. They gave me a socket
And I looked in my pocket.
The rocket landed on the planet Mars.
There were Mars Bars everywhere,
There was a chocolate factory
I could not believe my eyes
I saw Charlie and the Chocolate Factory
I think I've gone back in the past.
The last thing I saw was chocolate
I ate too much. I was sick.
But I kept picking all sorts of chocolate
The Space Girls said it was time to go back
I got in the rocket, I threw away the socket
And zoomed back.
Flash. On the computer chair again
Mum said, 'Do you want a Mars Bar?'

Lauren Carthy (8)
Stoke Poges School

STARS IN MY EYES

When I am zooming in space
I always see stars in my eyes
Stars in my eyes
Which make you lie
Stars in my eyes
Which make you bright.
One by one
I count the stars
1, 2, 3
Here we go!

Satwinder Sandhu (9)
Stoke Poges School

IN THE THIRD DIMENSION

I'm on a Euro-Star rocket to a space base,
Its name is Venus IV,
I've just come into space!
I'm going to travel to Jupiter!
I hope there's a big computer!
I'll head to Jupiter's great red spot
But beware of the Mackintocks!
You might get a bit of a knock!
If you get into trouble
Give them a crock to nibble!
But beware even more of their great
Ting, Tong, Dare!
Give them a pear,
It'll make them comb their hair!
If they have any!

Michael Potter (9)
Stoke Poges School

Up, Up And Away

Up goes the rocket
Into the dark night sky
Down on Earth
As we wave goodbye.

Up, up, up the rocket goes
Past Uranus and Pluto and goodness knows
When at last
They land on Mars

They found some aliens
That looked like Ford Escort cars
Their little dog Jack gave a bark
'Success,' said the man called Mark

The aliens said, 'Whoosh, whoosh, whoo.'
And the astronauts said, 'Who are you?'
Then all of a sudden up popped a king
I think he wants your golden ring.

Run, run, run to our spaceship quick
Quick he might blast our ship
Whoosh! Zoom! Back down to Earth
Past Venus and Pluto and a new planet Merth

When they arrived back at home
They had to give their hair a comb
You see it had been pulled up
From their flight back
And so had their little dog Jack.

Emily Bunby (8)
Stoke Poges School

OFF I GO!

Last night I went to the moon,
I zoomed up in the air.
I left my hair.
There were a lot of stars.
I felt hungry so I had some Mars bars
It was peaceful
And beautiful.

I got to the other side.
There was a big ride.
They took me to Jupiter.
There was a big rock.
The alien only had one sock.

It was time to go.
We went past Mars, Pluto
And then all the stars.
We had to stop at my bedroom window.

Avneet Kaur Badyal (8)
Stoke Poges School

THE BEAUTY OF SPACE

The sun is for happiness warm and bright,
Smiling faces at the sight.
The sun is children at a fairground,
Whizzing round on a merry-go-round.

The moon is calm, its meaning is love,
Just like a wedding happening above.
The moon has beauty like a silver ring,
Moving gently like a white dove's wing.

The stars mean a mystery far, far away,
They look like fireflies in the Milky Way.
The stars are diamonds flying free,
The stars really mean a lot to me.

And when I looked out my window,
And saw this other world.
I knew without the beauty of space,
The world would be a sadder place.

Rosanna Messer Stalbow (8)
Stoke Poges School

How Blip Lied To Ross

There was once a slimy alien called Blip,
Who had a big cut in his lip.
He had a friend called Ross,
Who thought he was the boss
Blip had a large spaceship he never used.
It was lime green, red and blue.
He called it white moon,
Because it lit up at noon.
As it was noon Blip the alien said,
'I'll go for a ride.'
He went for a long ride in his spaceship.
When Blip the alien came back,
He had bought a yellow Mac,
Ross the boss asked, 'Where did you just go for all that time?'
Blip the alien said, 'We ran out of lime.'
But really Blip the alien went to Mercury, Venus, Earth,
Mars, Jupiter, Saturn, Uranus, Neptune and Pluto.
He also came all the way back.
And that is how Blip lied to Ross.

Amritraj Sandhu (9)
Stoke Poges School

Cosmic Poem

I'm going into space
To the moon and the
stars and every place.
Met an alien on the
way and we had a little
play. Back in the spaceship,
Back to Earth,
landed in England for
all it was worth.

Elliot Noble (8)
Stoke Poges School

Aliens

There are green slimy aliens
Long ones, small ones and
fat ones.
They are flying down to earth
to eat all the teachers
They turn into children to catch
them out!
They have long green tentacles
and like to eat humans.
They have three eyes, three legs, four arms
and spectacles.

Kesia Foulsham (9)
Stoke Poges School

DEEP SPACE

There was a planet called Mars
I discovered it had lots of cars
Made from chocolate bars
There was an alien teacher
Who had a funny feature
It was a weird creature
All of the aliens in space
Are having a race
First comes Ross the Boss
Second comes Skinny
Third comes Fat
With his bat
And his cat
And that's the end of that.

Marc Byne (9)
Stoke Poges School

SPACE GIRLS

Space Girls are jumping and flying,
Pouncing off air
And dancing like mad.
Air girls.
Space girls.
Good space people and bad.
Clever girls and silly ones
Dancing ones too.
Eating girls.
Whatever next?

Katie Russell (8)
Stoke Poges School

Stars In Your Eyes And Planets

S pace I'm talking about space,
T winkling stars in your eyes,
A planet turning like a dancer,
R ocket zooming up,
S tars in your eyes

I 'm going to space,
N ice universe we have got

Y ou are so angry because I'm going to space,
O ur world is our world
U mbrella! I need an umbrella it's raining,
R ain going down from space

E T come down my brother's gone mad!
Y ou are so angry
E T come down my family's gone mad,
S tars in your eyes

A funny creature there,
N ow! Blast off. I'm going to the stars,
D ad let me go to space

P lanets, planets,
L ady press the button!
A funny human!
N ice universe again,
E verybody cheers for me
T oday hello, bye for now,
S hall see you soon in space.

Belinda Kaur Bal (8)
Stoke Poges School

THE NEW ALIEN

In the night
When it's very dark,
The new alien appeared
And his dog gave a bark.
He looked through the window
And then got a scare
There was a sign that said,
Beware
He went down the steps
With his pet dog
Then out popped a Martian
Who said, 'My name's Mog.'
'Oh go away
Leave me alone
Before I whack you
With my dog's bone!'
'Oh little fellow
Do calm down
How about I take you
To an alien town?'
He jumped on the planets
One by one,
He thought he was having
Lots of fun.
Then he got a sudden slip
He had fallen in a big deep dip.
In the dip he caught the flu
But don't worry this isn't true!

Krista Pettit (8)
Stoke Poges School

The Aliens From Jupiter

Rockets go whoosh!
Earth and Mars tremble
As the terrifying aliens come.
The aliens arrive
Crashed by my side
At the other side of Mars.
But not the Mars that are chocolate bars.
The sun flamed and burned the aliens.
The aliens got a terrible fright and jumped
Up and down till they were out of sight.
The aliens went off through dark stormy night
And then came back with a big black sack.
They opened the sack and there was a big attack
And that was the end of that.

Amrita Nijjar (9)
Stoke Poges School

Rocket Power

Rocket flying in the sky
Looming past, the stars say 'Bye.'
It flies past the planets
So it does not know where to go
In the early afternoon it landed on a small moon
The astronaut opened the door
And put his foot on the floor
He looked around in dark space
And then he saw an ugly face.
An alien with yellow hair
And eyes that glared.
On the moon I saw some turf
I saw my ship and left for earth.

James Galvin (9)
Stoke Poges School

Shooting Stars

Once there was a spaceship
it was really, really big.
It had a net about the size of a jumbo jet
For catching bits and bobs.
The ship was full of aliens
Slimy and gungy
Their antennae were about two metres long
They didn't reach the ceiling
But they nearly reached the light.

They ate fried mouse and a brick of a house
They were coloured green just like
A rotten baked bean
They drank some wine
With a pinch of horrible slime.

Daniel Kiddle (9)
Stoke Poges School

5, 4, 3, 2, 1 Blast Off

Five . . . go into the rocket.
Four . . . do your belt up.
Three . . listen to the radio.
Two . . . start the engine.
One . . . get ready for blast off.
Blast-Off!

Gary De-Ville (8)
Stoke Poges School

Planets

Jupiter is a huge gas ball.
Pluto is small.
Saturn is big with swirling rocks around it all,
Mercury's the hottest and you'll soon find out
When you travel close to it you'll have no doubt,
Earth is where we live,
Sun is our heat,
Mars has got thin air,
Venus is a middle sized planet you know what I mean,
Neptune's one of the biggest,
Uranus is shaped like a ball.
That's all of the planets
I hope you like them all.

Edward Barton (8)
Stoke Poges School

The Man In Space

There was a man in space,
Who went at his own pace,
He didn't like the stars,
That's why he ended up on Mars,
He went to Saturn,
He lost his picture pattern.

Charlene Willis (10)
Stoke Poges School

THE MOON'S FACE

5, 4, 3, 2, 1 . . . Blast Off.
We're taking off away from Earth to land upon the moon.
We've landed. I felt it.
It felt like silver silk.
It smelt like a rose as it went through my nose.
My mum was the stars and my dad is Mars.
I'm alone on the moon.
Nobody cares.
Only my teddy cares.
I'm lonely like a lost baboon.
I get in my rocket and off I whiz.
Whoosh, I'm in my rocket.
I can see the moon shining white.
What a beautiful sight.

Katie Oldfield (8)
Stoke Poges School

THE EARTH

The universe is an enormous place.
Where planets, moons and stars are.
They seem to be all the same
Except for Earth which is on its own.
It's where humans live
That's what makes it different.

Matthew Robinson (9)
Stoke Poges School

Space

The Sun
The sun is my mum
She is very calm
She gives me light
Day and night
Then hides away
Out of sight.

Planets and Stars
Planets and stars
All rhyme with Mars
The aliens in space,
Give stars a race.
The aliens are also weird
They have eyes on stalks
And tentacle ears.

Man in the Moon
Did you know
The Man in the Moon
Used to whistle and hum,
And when he got bored
he would beat his drum.

The Milky Way
I looked through my
Telescope once
And saw a beautiful boat
it was sailing across the
Milky Way
I don't know how it
stayed afloat.

Joanna Milne (8)
Stoke Poges School

THE ALIEN CALLED STARS

On the planet Mars,
There is a wet slimy alien called Stars.
He has a big spaceship called Blimp,
It is red, green and pink.
All day long Stars sits around and eats,
All he ever eats is sweets.
Sometimes at the weekend he goes out in his spaceship.
To get into his spaceship you have to undo the zip.
One day at the weekend Stars flew to the moon,
Whilst he was flying to the moon,
In his spaceship he found a spoon.
He was looking at the spoon,
And he crashed into the moon
And that was the end of Stars.

Lauren Burford (9)
Stoke Poges School

PLANETS

Super rockets up in space.
Pounding around in their base.
As you look in stars.
Come and see the Milky Bars,
Even you could be the lucky one!

On my way to space,
1, 2, 3, 4, 5, 6, 7, 8, 9, 10
We're off
But my rocket got left behind.
So I went down, down and bang!
Well wouldn't you know!
I landed in a dustbin *boom, boom, bang!*

Christopher Venning (9)
Stoke Poges School

The Canderalet

I was in space,
It was the colour of a black case,
I saw Mars,
Million times bigger than Mars Bars.

I landed.

I got out the ship,
Which was nearly in bits,
I walked round the planet,
There in surprise was a *Canderalet!*
It was an *Alien!*
The size of Verulamuim,
I ran back to the ship,
But it was in bits,
The alien blasted me back to Earth.

Tristan Blackie (8)
Stoke Poges School

Missing

M issing from the universe
I nsulation pipe cut off and all hope's lost.
S omersaulting off course.
S cared to death of losing his life.
I magining his wife and children.
N o hope of getting his boosters working.
G oing, going, going, gone . . .

Marcus Johns (9)
Stoke Poges School

Flying Through Space

Whizzing, shooting, whoosh, bang!
Flying through space is fun,
All in silence with stars all around.
Mars is beautiful with its ring of gold.
It has beautiful colours of red, blue and orange mixed
in wonderfully.
Whizzing, shooting, whoosh, bang!
Flying through space is fun.
Now we're flying over Jupiter.
With its bright orange coat.
Isn't it beautiful, doesn't it sparkle?
Whizzing, shooting, whoosh, bang!
Flying through space is fun.
Mercury is wonderful
With its lovely shade of blue.
It's a wonderful experience
Whizzing, shooting, whoosh, bang!
Flying through space is fun.
Venus is a beautiful place
It's colour is red, dark, dark red.
I'm glad I came out today.
Whizzing, shooting, whoosh, bang!
Flying through space is fun.
'Get off my sofa now!'
'Yes Mum!'
Well it was fun while it lasted!

Katie Duncombe (9)
Stoke Poges School

THE STAR

Sparkling in the sky
Tracing it up so high,
Away and near the moon
Rockets see it now and soon.

Joanna Susan Peters (9)
Stoke Poges School

ISLAND POEM

One sandy hot day
I went to the jungle
And I had an adventure
An alligator came out
And I found a stick
In its mouth.

Michael Logan (6)
The Hawthorns Primary School

ISLAND POEM

One day on an island
It was very hot
So I wore a crop top
And shorts because . . .
It was very hot
So I drank the milk
From a coconut.

Nadia Leathes (6)
The Hawthorns Primary School

Island Poem

One blazing sandy day
I saw my hot air balloon
And shouted, 'Hooray!'
All the trees
Were swaying like mad
And one hit me
Very bad!

Nathan Elcox (6)
The Hawthorns Primary School

Island Poem

On a dry desert island
There were some funny things
Like parakeets and bumble bees
I find them very funny
They do strange things.
But there are dangerous things
Like sharks and snakes.

Gregg Allison (7)
The Hawthorns Primary School

Island Poem

One hot day
I tried to push
My boat
Into the water
And a shark came!

Celeste Griffiths (7)
The Hawthorns Primary School

ISLAND POEM

In the jungle
Steamy and hot
Don't go there
There's danger!
Tarantulas, tigers
As well as snakes
Please don't go there
It's dangerous.

Jessica Crandon (7)
The Hawthorns Primary School

TOMORROW

Tomorrow we're getting a new pet,
It's going to be a guinea-pig but . . .
We don't know what to call it yet.
My sister said that we should call it Joe,
But the rest of us just don't know.

We are going to play with it every day,
Instead of playing in the hay.
We are all squabbling over who's cleaning it.
I said that I would as long as I get pocket money
Because normally they all forget, that's why I haven't got any yet!

They all said that it was fine,
So they all went and had a glass of wine.
Then soon it was time for bed,
Unless we stay up and have a feast instead!
Shhhhh!

Laura Miller (10)
Uplands Primary School

My Best Friend

My best friend is called Rog,
He snores like a wart hog,
But Mum wants to get rid of him,
And put him in the bin.

My best friend has ears like pigs,
And has 30 red wigs.
My best friend is an artist,
And all he ever thinks about is the shopping list.

My best friend plays with me,
Five minutes after tea.
My best friend likes to have a stroll in the park,
My best friend is a troll with a bark!

Holly Yapp (10)
Uplands Primary School

My Best Friend

My best friend is short and shabby.
My best friend is very small.
My best friend talks a lot.
I always take him ice skating.
I never learn a thing at school.
I always listen to him.
He fits in my pocket.
I change the channel when he gets boring.
He tells me everything that goes on in the world.
My best friend's a Walkman.

Christopher Hammersley (9)
Uplands Primary School

My Best Friend

My best friend comes from Mars
and not surprisingly he eats Mars bars.
My best friend is very small,
he can't even kick a ball.

My little Walkman can't fit his head,
even an ant is as small as his bed.
My best friend drives a racing car.
My best friend has drinks at the bar.

My best friend likes walking down the street,
his favourite cereal is Shredded Wheat.
My best friend likes riding on cars.
My best friend is Mighty Max!

Alex Todd (10)
Uplands Primary School

My Best Friend

My best friend is this
My best friend is that
My best friend is me
My best friend is Pat
Is he fat or is he slim?
We'll never know, he is my best friend.
My best friend is thin
My best friend is me
My best friend is a pen
My best friend is me.

Lee Burnett (11)
Uplands Primary School

TOMORROW

Tomorrow I'm going to Canada,
To see the lovely things there.
Then I'm off to Egypt,
To see the ancient tombs.

Then I'm off to France,
To taste the lovely shortcakes.
Then I'm off to Dublin,
To have a short break.

Then I'm off to New York
To have a short holiday of my own.
Greece sounds like a nice place,
Better go there next term.

Then at last my final stop is Italy,
What do they have there?
But I think I'm better off home,
I imagine what it's like in the air.

Jade Iehec Watson (10)
Uplands Primary School

MY BEST FRIEND

My best friend is very, very special,
She gives me things that are nice and beautiful,
She can be loud but not as loud as me,
We wish that we were family.

Karen is afraid of big, big dogs,
She's not as loud when she sees my dog,
When we get older we want to live together, her and me,
But we still wish that we were family.

Kelly Head (10)
Uplands Primary School

My Best Friends

My best friend is sort of small
The other one is very tall
I am the middle size of them all
But I am not the best at football!

Every Thursday we go to the park
And every Thursday we kill a lark . . . in the park
At school we play pogs with the frogs
And we never, ever, never, ever get into mischief
I hope!

My other friends are not so nice
Because they're out with yuk! Baby Spice
There's a girl in our class who is always happy
I don't know why she is so happy
Maybe she is happy because something's gone right
Or is it because she is very bright?
Now I've got to run
Because the baker's got a free bun!

Aaron Morgan (9)
Uplands Primary School

My Best Friend

Guess who my best friend is?
She's the best in the whole world.
She's also very kind.

Hey you better beware!
Or she'll be after you.
Because she loves playing games.

She plays around,
And watches TV.
She lets you stay up late!
And loves CBBC.

Do you know yet?
I'll tell you so,
It's my mum.

Charlotte Rough (10)
Uplands Primary School

MY BEST FRIEND

My best friend has brown eyes.
When my friend falls over she
Sometimes cries.
She has blond hair
and she never does a dare,
she sometimes eats pears.

My best friend has lots
of colouring pens.
She also likes hens.
She likes art
and she like jam tarts.
Natalie Cobbett is my best friend.

She likes reading magazines,
she likes music as well.
Her favourite group is Boyzone,
but she doesn't like beetroot.
She also likes dolphins.
My best friend is Natalie Cobbett.

Amiirah Joommun (10)
Uplands Primary School

My Best Friend

My best friend is my mum
She is always nice and kind
My best friend is my mum
My homework diary is always signed.

My mum has dark brown hair
She has pretty clothes too
My mum is always fair
My mum has never had the flu.

My mum has blue, blue eyes
My mum is married to dad
My mum, she never cries
My mum, she's never bad.

Mikayla Field (9)
Uplands Primary School

Tomorrow

Tomorrow I'm going into space,
I don't know if there is such a place.

I'm going by bike,
If there's a spike.

I'm going to Mars,
With a pass.

Back at home my brother's playing,
With my dad, he's paying.

With my mum,
I have lots of fun.

Lucy Fuller (9)
Uplands Primary School

Tomorrow

Tomorrow I'm getting a new pet
I think it's a Tyrannosaurus Rex
But I don't think they have them in stock
They're rather an unusual choice.

Tomorrow I'm going to the sweet shop
I think I'm going to get some pick and mix
But I might get a Twix
But I might decide to get a toy.

Tomorrow I'm going to watch TV
While I'm having my tea
And then I'm going to watch TV
And then I'm going down the shops with ten p.

Daniel Smith (10)
Uplands Primary School

My Best Friend

My best friend is very funny
My best friend likes honey
My best friend has a brother
My best friend loves his mother

My best friend is quite small
My best friend is good at football
My best friend has blond hair
My best friend plays truth or dare

My best friend wears glasses made of glass
My best friend is not the fastest in the class
My best friend is ten years old
My best friend is called Daniel.

Thomas Evans (10)
Uplands Primary School

My Best Friend

My best friend is called Abby Turner
She is crazy and funny and a party animal
She sings and dances and watches TV
and clicks her fingers and slaps her knee.

She has a dog and one goldfish
She has blond hair and hazel eyes
Her house is big, her garden's small
and her dog chases her round it with a ball.

She likes art and the park
and that's why she's my friend
She has a sister who's older than her
and goes to secondary school.

Natalie Cobbett (10)
Uplands Primary School

My Best Friend

My best friend
Drives me round the bend
She winds me up and up
She has light brown hair and
has a very cute teddy bear and
plays with me a lot.

My best friend likes make-up
She likes nail varnish too
She wears pretty dresses and
eats lots of biscuits and
nice yummy chocolates too.

Ashley Jones (10)
Uplands Primary School

Tomorrow

Tomorrow I'm going to the moon
and on a flying teaspoon!
Don't worry I've tested it out,
and it takes me here and about.

And when I want to take it somewhere,
it will always be here,
but if it's not,
it will always be there!

And on the flying teaspoon
everyone wants to come!
and I think I know why
Because it's so much fun!

And plus going to the moon is so much fun
but on the flying teaspoon
It's even more fun!

So defiantly ride on the flying teaspoon,
you will not get cross!
and I promise you that
because on the flying teaspoon,
you go wherever you want!

So come on the flying teaspoon!

Daniel Deller-Twinney (10)
Uplands Primary School

TOMORROW

Tomorrow I just want to stay in bed,
But I just can't because I'll be dead.
I go to my friend's house to go to school
And we walk so I'm rather chilly and cool.

When I get there I am totally drenched,
I get inside and my teeth are clenched.
My teacher says 'Line up for assembly.'
When I line up I'm rather trembly.

Then she said I had to stay behind,
And then I thought she was out of her mind!
Luckily it was only for reading,
She must have been really needing.

Then everybody comes back,
It would be quicker going on a hack.
After that we changed for maths,
Then it sounded like flying bats.

Georgina Brown (10)
Uplands Primary School

MY BEST FRIEND

My best friend is Patrick
he scored the winning hat trick.
The football match was cool
because Daniel dressed as a fool.

The next day we went to school
Daniel was still dressed up as a fool.
Next week my friend Patrick scored
another hat trick and Daniel was still
dressed up as a fool.

Luke Groves (9)
Uplands Primary School

Tomorrow

Tomorrow I'll go to London,
To see what there is there.
Then I'll go to Canada,
To see a grizzly bear.

Then I'll be in Mexico,
To try the spicy food.
Tomorrow I'm in Dublin,
To see Boyzone there.

Then I'll be home,
For a little while.
Then guess where I'll be?
In New Zealand to see the kiwis.

Tomorrow I'm in New York,
To go shopping there.
Then I'm in France,
To taste some slimy snails.

Tomorrow I'm in Spain,
To see some dancing there.
Then I'll be in England,
Relaxing in a chair.

Laura Cobbett (10)
Uplands Primary School

MY KITE

My kite is like a peacock
on a ball of string,
flying around the sky.
My kite is like a hawk
diving for his prey.
My kite is like an owl
in the night fall.
My kite is like a gull
whirling, round and round.
My kite is like a crow
pacing to and fro.
My kite is like a kestrel
racing through the sky.
My kite is like a jay
looking for berries.

Amy Lack (10)
Waverley School

THE CLOCK

A clock tells the time
like a big watch
A clock ticks
like a teacher
marking good work
A clock has two hands
like me
A clock keeps going
like a good runner.

Andrew Sinclair (10)
Waverley School

Dogs

The dog is as fast as a boy on his bike.
It is as bushy as a bush with hair.
They can bite, but,
they have muzzles,
and they have a lot of muscles!
They eat a lot,
they even eat honey out of a pot!
Dogs are very strong,
just like King Kong!
Dogs are sweet and cuddly too.
Some of them are small,
some of them are tall,
and they come to you
when you call.

Matthew Edwards (9)
Waverley School

The Fence

The fence by the playground
Keeps us from freedom,
It's like a soldier,
Keeping us from the playing field.
A soldier, as solid as a locked door,
When the keys have been
Thrown away.

Paul Stephenson (10)
Waverley School

ADVENT

The coming of Jesus is a joyful time
A time to remember,
When Mary had Jesus
This joyful time of December.
We light our candles
To show our joy,
The celebration
Of the baby boy.
We light our candles
They are so bright
And shine out
In the darkness of the night.
Christmas is coming very fast
Happy children
Are hoping Santa will go past.
It is the Advent of the year
Shining candles are so clear.
In December it gets terribly dark
But you can hear angels singing,
Hark!
The coming of Jesus is a joyful time
A time to remember,
When Mary had Jesus
This joyful time of December.

Faye Hetherington (9)
Waverley School

The Snail

A snail is
sliming,
climbing,
sticking to the wall.
Climbing up very high
as high as a tall
building
in the sky.
He will never stop
until he gets to the top
where he needs to get.
Still sliming,
climbing,
sticking to the wall.

Jay McCafferty (9)
Waverley School

The Killer Whale

The tail
smashes against the sea,
as brilliant as fireworks
going up into the sky.
The black and white markings
look as clear as the sky
on a sunny day.
The size
is as big as a dragon.

Caroline Hoad (10)
Waverley School

The Full Moon

The full moon is a beach ball,
being thrown up into the sky.
People are playing volley ball,
hitting it really high.
It's going so high
into the sky.
No one can see it,
floating up high.
It shoots up very fast,
when it is night,
even though it's out of sight,
and comes down in the morning.

Rosanna Van Reyk (10)
Waverley School

My Kite

My kite is like a bird,
flying up into the sky,
swooping, ducking
and riding thermal air.
Twisting and turning
and yearning for more.
Until, it slowly glides
back to earth again.

Hayden Taylor (10)
Waverley School

My Pets

I have three cats.
Their names are
Ebony,
Bobby
and Patch.
Ebony is black,
Bobby is black and white,
and Patch is tortoise-shell.
Ebony's always looking out of the window,
Bobby's lazy, always asleep,
and Patch is playful and cuddly.
They always come to me,
mornings and nights.

Katrina House (9)
Waverley School

My Brother

My brother is annoying,
He just won't go away,
He pulls my hair and tricks me,
He doesn't even let me play!

We shouted at one another,
For a single day,
Until my angry mother
Came and sent us both away!

Bethany Mallac (10)
Waverley School

STABLES

Early morning at the stables,
it's a very busy time.
You can hear all the horses,
stamping their feet,
waiting to be fed.
You can see, and feel,
the soft fur,
the crunching and the neighing,
the smell of food,
all mixed with the country air.

Late at night,
when it gets dark,
the quieter it is.
The only noise you can hear
is the miaowing of the cat,
chasing mice.
You can smell the leather
in the tack room.
The tap is dripping,
gently,
into the bucket.
Later,
you could hear
a pin drop.

Clare Hawthorn (9)
Waverley School

Animals

Animals may be strong, they maybe weak,
We may only see them at a peek,
They really are like nature's gifts,
Some are pets, some are wild,
Some are simply very mild.
Lions stalk, with a sway,
While cheetahs run their very own way.
Every pet lives a lifetime,
While African animals are shot,
As a prize for their spots.

Craig Nightingale (10)
Waverley School

Space

The new moon is a clump of cheese,
Sparkling
Amongst some dark blue candyfloss,
Floating across the sky,
Mars - a hot balloon blazing,
Pluto - a blue sponge of paint,
Freezing
Cold
Waiting to be explored.

Gemma Bray (9)
Waverley School

The Kite

High in the sky,
it hovers,
as silently as a hawk
looking for its prey.
High in the sky,
it hovers silently,
looking for its prey.
The kite is a hawk,
hunting for his prey.

Philip Blincow (10)
Waverley School

Moon

There he stands staring down
Pulling at the shivering waves
Watching all that passes by
As nobody looks at him
Dying away.

But soon
As darkness falls upon his body
His life arrives again
No longer that fragile decrepit vase
But an exquisite and powerful tycoon.

The sun is his servant
And she reinforces his power
To make his gleam of silver
Seem like a channel of jewels
As a knight in shining armour.

Kavanjot Benepal (9)
Wexham Court Primary School

THE MOON

The moon is round
it shines like a star
but really the sun is her supporter.
The night changes slowly
but she spills her liquid silver.
There are full moons, half moons too.
Sometimes dull, sometimes radiant.
The moon flows with the clouds
  Then
    Freezes
      Like
        A
          Statue
            Still.

Katie Hutchinson (9)
Wexham Court Primary School

MOON

Moon is always the same, she never dies
Then she
          D
            A
              N
                C
                  E
                    S

With the stars in the night light sky
As soon as animals go to sleep, out she comes
And she lights up the night sky like
A bright light. Her full moon.

Kirsty Keohane (10)
Wexham Court Primary School

Moon

In the satisfied sky,
the moon is shining high,
high upon us,
nightly.
The moon is light
like a large glowing, gleaming
star,
and like illuminated
dancing comets.
The sun will support him
when it's dark.
His strength is gathered.
In the morning
he's in a bed of needles
so he's gone
like an invisible ghost
that you can't see
until the
next day.

Stuart Webb (9)
Wexham Court Primary School

In The Distance

In the distance I see
Bare trees slowly
Moving in the breeze.

I watch the birds
Fly in groups,
Gripping onto their tiny roots.

I look deeply into the trees
Then see some ripe green fields
With the sun shining high above them.

As the clouds slowly pass by,
I see that the shining sun
Is no longer high.

Noor Al-Basri (10)
Wexham Court Primary School

Moon

Magically, mysteriously moving moon
Making its way through a typhoon
The faces of the meekly moon
Are all strange and weird
Silently moving round and round
Magically moving across the sky
Magnificently standing there
and shining humorously
Fighting sun and cloud
She returns once more
Blocking his heat
Hourly shining
The sun he fights back
And wins
She is gone
She shall return
And die once more
For the sun
He will win once more.

Scott Perry (10)
Wexham Court Primary School

NIGHT

At night I hear owls hooting
and see bats swooping . . .
I lie there thinking what might
be under my bed.

I look out the window
and I see the moon
There are mysterious noises
I think there's a ghost in my house.

Shadows on the walls and doors
Shadows on the floor
Shadows *everywhere!*
I put my head under my pillow
and go to sleep.

Holly Cook (10)
Wexham Court Primary School

I WONDER IF THERE ARE ALIENS

I wonder if there are aliens
On Mars, Jupiter or maybe the sun
It would be so nice to meet one
They may be pink, they may be green
I wonder if there are aliens

I wonder if there are aliens
Hopefully they would be nice and
Not bad like other ones
It would be so nice to meet one
I wonder if there are aliens.

Rebecca Horth (9)
Wexham Court Primary School

MOON

She's like a penny turning
Shining silver nightly
The clouds blanch her colour
She becomes invisible
but when it is dark
the moon gathers light
for herself to use
but when it
                    is
                      gone
she vanishes out of sight!

She is the queen
The stars bow down before her
They do what she orders
otherwise they're gone!
The stars shine brightly
but not as bright as her.

Charis Wilcox (10)
Wexham Court Primary School

MY PUPPY

I love my puppy, he's just like a brother.
We have really good fun when we play together.
Run round the garden, chase the ball.
Who's the first to reach the wall?
When we've stopped playing, it's time for a rest.
And puppy has his dinner, that's what he likes best.
Asleep by the fire, his head on my knee.
We're happy together just puppy and me.

Natalie Green (8)
Wexham Court Primary School

MOON

Moon, moon
How far do you go?
Please tell me moon

Moon, moon
You look like a night in shining armour
The moon is a magic mystery light

Moon, moon
Playing in the sky
Dancing with the stars

Moon, moon
You're like a large circle
Just sitting there.

Torren Dalton (10)
Wexham Court Primary School

MOON

Sometimes corpulent
Sometimes lean, sometimes like an orange skin
The sun is the man
The moon is his lady
The stars are the children in the sky
The silver lady dances across the sky
They glow in the night, but in the morning they are *gone.*

Katrina Goodman (10)
Wexham Court Primary School

Moon

In the silent, sophisticated night
As the heavenly bodies, stars, look down on us,
The magical, mysterious moon
Arises
Lit up by the sun
In its wizardry ways
Like a conjurer
Conjuring up a new spell
It changes form
Its figure transforms, alters
The immense moonlight gathers
As the moon guides its stars
As it lights up the world
In its devilish ways
The luminous moon lives again.

Jasdeep Mondae (9)
Wexham Court Primary School

My Pond

The water glistened in the sun's rays
The fish basked in their lazy ways.
The cat purred then ran and played
The frog hopped from pebble to pebble then stayed.
This is my pond on spring days.

Phillip Binge (7)
Wexham Court Primary School

THE HUNT

The orange figure bounds across the meadows full of fear
not knowing how long he can last,
his eyes burn with the fear of death,
his tail slags as he stops to listen for the devilish beasts,
they are upon him,
a shadow falls around him,
as dogs move in he bounds away
they chase him,
his ears hang low and his strength is slowly dying.
In a last effort he sinks down in the undergrowth.
this graceful creature is at last beaten.
After hunting for food this creature has been hunted down.
Why must these devils kill?
At last they move in and the dogs pounce.
Then silence.

David Calder (11)
Owlsmoor Primary School

DEATH SONG

The wailing song of death fills the air,
As the murderous destructors drop whistling bombs,
With the hand of death closely behind.
As each life-taker whistles to the ground,
The hand of death swoops down and snatches at the souls of
the victims.
Guns shoot again and again but have no effect.
The relieving all-clear sounds,
And everyone is delighted for it is over for now.

Kevin Underwood (10)
Owlsmoor Primary School

The Deadly Hunter

It has killed lamb and goat,
It has poached chicken and hare,
It has tortured the innocent.

The hunt is moving left and right,
Over and under, in and out.

The reason why he kills is not to be blamed,
He needs to eat, he needs to live,
But the hunter kills for no reason.

Who is right, who is wrong?
Both are mean, both are strong.

But the huntsman is stronger in number,
He will demand his way,
The fox is weak compared to them.

Death is near for the hunted huntsman,
He will kill no more.

The fear in his eyes shows he is weak,
And he will run no more.

James Jarvis (10)
Owlsmoor Primary School

Thoughts In The Air Raid Shelter

When will the wild song of death come to us?
When will the big black devils put out the light in our sky?
When will this war end?
Who will win?
No one!

Jake Smith (11)
Owlsmoor Primary School

My Poem On The Blitz

Murderous eagles searching ever endlessly for prey,
Searching, searching for death to satisfy their hunger.
Frightened mice scatter quickly into their metal shelters,
Pearl-white searchlights stripe the sky in search of
predatory eagles.
A blanket of fear and evil covers the city of fire.
Eventually the silent mice climb and stumble out of
metal shelters,
For their tearful eyes to meet a fire-ravaged and
unrecognisable scene,
The death and destruction is over for now, but
tomorrow . . . ?

Emily Hanson-Coles (10)
Owlsmoor Primary School

Memories Last Longer Than Life

Suddenly the air was full of smoke,
For gas was drifting, making soldiers choke.
Rat-infested, torn-up ground,
Soldiers lying there, not making a sound.
The war was over, too many were dead,
For all that was left, one lonesome poppy, red.
At last silence had taken place
And grandparents were pulling a sad, devastated face.
Memories last longer than life!

Jason Barker (11)
Owlsmoor Primary School

The Air Raid

The wailing siren sending a warning,
Terrified people hurry into their damp shelters,
Waiting silently for it to begin,
The first murderous explosion makes the ground tremble,
Another life-threatening bomb plummets down,
A family scream as their cramped shelter is hit,
The relief when the all-clear drones,
But the devastating sight of lifeless bodies is heartbreaking,
Nothing will ever be the same.

Olivia Shenton-Taylor (11)
Owlsmoor Primary School

The Air Raid

I looked up in the blackened sky,
Searchlights were probing for the bombers from hell.
Would they send their life-taking cargo crashing to the ground?
Destroying people and their cheaply built homes.
Yes!
Houses demolished, exploding with fire.
Then the British who'd survived emerged from beneath,
Looking at the devastation the evil had left.

Keri Parkinson (10)
Owlsmoor Primary School

THE BLITZ

As the siren wails its wail of fear,
A state of panic crosses London.
People rush hurriedly to their shelters,
Panic becomes silence.
The life-taking bombs dropping from a height bring fear
to the streets,
Fire breaks out in every corner of the city,
Caved in crushed houses lay in a rubble heap on the ground,
The evil Hitler and his bomber planes have once again brought
terror to London.
Will tomorrow bring our death?

Sam Stockley (11)
Owlsmoor Primary School

THE VOLCANO

The sea erupts like a volcano,
Shooting, spurting out with all its might.
Pounding over the rocks like a hungry bear,
Cascading over the pier like it never cares.
But as the volcano stops pelting,
And the waves stop striking,
The sun shimmers on the sparkling blue ripples
In the peaceful sea.

Jennifer Mahoney (11)
Wooden Hill Primary School

THE ROUGH SEA

The sea foams and clashes against the rocks;
Hurling giant rocks smash with the sea,
Distant grey sky clouds over,
The rough sea strikes again,
Terrorising the sand and cliff faces,
Scattering rocks and sand;
Stunning light shines through the cracks - glaring;
Gold layers of sand sitting alone,
Colours of the sky blend in;
The pier lurches as the waves smash against it,
Clanging boulders storm to the sea as it races about.

Emma Duncombe (10)
Wooden Hill Primary School

AS CALM AS THE SEA

As the sun lowers itself behind the cliff edge,
Waves bob up and down.
Silently splashes and sploshes
Appear on the delicate waves.
One by one tiny pebbles
Fall from the rocky front.
The wind hums
While the waves lap
Until no more pebbles fall.

Holly Wilson (10)
Wooden Hill Primary School

The Sea

The sea is like a playful dog,
Shooting round the rocks,
Smashing and crashing over the coral,
Evening light dawns on the sea
As the sky turns red and orange,
And the clouds go lilac and purple.
The playful dog turns soft and quiet
So all you can hear is a gentle ripple
As sea comes into shore.

Linda Moore (11)
Wooden Hill Primary School

The Quiet Sea

The quiet sea, sparkling in the sun,
With its wavy action
Like a baby sleeping in the golden sea.
It's stunning and beautiful,
With its dark and light colours mixed,
With its rocky shore
And its shiny effect.
With the sun gleaming through it
I just wish I was really there.

Louise Doyle (11)
Wooden Hill Primary School

THE PURPLE SEA

The purple sea shines brightly
In the sunset,
Dark and light colours all mixed into one.
The sky is like an artist's palette streaking the sky.
It's still, quiet
Nobody to be seen.
The stony rocks just sit there
All still and alone.
The sea sways backwards and forwards
Like it won't stay still,
Everything is sitting there
All sad and alone.

Katie Smith (10)
Wooden Hill Primary School

THE ULTRA GOLD RAY

The ocean as calm as a sloth climbing
The gods, walloping ultra gold rays at the ocean,
The jagged surface doing all it can to keep the ocean sloth down,
The orange clouds trying to cover the blinding sun.

Markos Stratford (10)
Wooden Hill Primary School